Retributive Justice and Ethics of Love relating to Rape Victim

Retributive Justice and Ethics of Love relating to Rape Victim

Jajo Somi

Christian World Imprints™

First Published in 2019 by

Christian World Imprints™
Christian Publishing & Books from India
H-12 Bali Nagar, **New Delhi-110015**
info@christianworldimprints.com
www.ChristianWorldImprints.com
Phone: +91 11 25465925

ISBN: 978-93-5148-316-8

Cataloging in Publication Data--DK
Courtesy: D.K. Agencies (P) Ltd. <docinfo@dkagencies.com>

Somi, Jajo, 1973- **author.**
Retributive justice and ethics of love relating to rape victim / Jajo Somi.
pages cm
Includes bibliographical references.
ISBN 9789351483168
1. Lex talionis--India. 2. Retribution--Religious aspects--Christianity. 3. Love--Religious aspects--Christianity. 4. Compensation (Law)--India. 5. Rape victims--India. 6. Rape--Religious aspects--Christianity. I. Title.

LCC BL65.R48S66 2019 | DDC 261.8336010954 23

Printed in India.

Contents

Foreword

This work is a welcome contribution to the lesser known and neglected discourse on retributive justice and love in the light of Christian ethics. The work is being published at an appropriate time when the incidences of rape have been increasing day after day. The publication is also timely where theological reflection and discourse on justice and love with reference to rape victim are not only scanty but a grey area of theological discourse.

Retributive justice is a relatively new discourse although the concept has been rooted for long. The theme transcends various disciplines although the approaches and orientations would differ from each other. As a discourse, the theme is largely associated with ethics, law and other disciplines of the social sciences. Theology has been one of the foremost disciplines that have been concerned with retributive justice. Among these theological realms, Christian theology has been considerably taking the lead in addressing justice.

Despite the relevance of the subject matter, no religion seems to seriously embark on the discourse of justice, or in the least, the space for discourse is either restricted or is not encouraged. Every religion seems to be holding the principle that (their) religion is a *sui generis* phenomenon, and therefore would avert from any discourse. Thus, by and large, one would observe the insistence of a static approach to religious discourse. This is one of the main reasons why the so-called religious authorities would even go to the extent of considering some scholars and/or believers as heretic for flouting new perspective/s on any of the dimensions of the belief system and practice.

In Christian theology, the discourse on retributive justice is not new. Many Christian groups, theologians and scholars have been debating on this theme as to whether or not retributive justice is biblical. There are some scholars who opine that retributive justice is a phenomenon of the pre-Christ era, and therefore, after the coming of Jesus Christ, there is no need for such kind of justice. However, there are many scholars who consider that retributive justice is biblically relevant. The argument has been largely based on the broad framework of *Penal Substitutionary Theory* (PST) of atonement. However, there seems to be lesser discourse on the relationship between retributive justice and love although some scholars have begun to throw perspectives. But there are much lesser works available on the application of this theory to rape victim.

In this book, the author throws perspective on what would be biblically sound to appropriate justice to the victim. He considers rape victims as a case to this discourse. In his discourse, he attempts to establish the relationship between retributive justice and love. He tries to co-relate the duo by using the broad framework of '*Christo-centric ethics*' proposed by Paul Ramsey.

The central arguments/theses of the author are mainly four-fold: First, there is a close relationship between retributive justice and love; Second, retributive justice is incomplete without the crucial element of love; Third, punishment and/or compensation for the crime should commensurate with the crime committed; and Fourth, the settlement of rape case should be with the consent of the victim and the offender where the former forgives the crime through love after genuine confession and appropriate compensation from the latter.

The author has chosen a discourse which is very relevant to the contemporary times. It is a crucial discourse for a country like India where discussions and debates are going on since the recent past as to how to deal with the offender and the victim of rape cases. It has become a great challenge to the society in addressing these issues because the phenomenon transcends into the individual, family and society at large.

The quintessence of the book shall drive home with the kind of response from the readers as to the soundness of its approach and perspectives. This piece of work will be useful to those scholars (theologians and secular scholars as well) and Christians in general who are concerned with the issue of rape case and its implications.

R. Vashum
New Delhi

Acknowledgment

It is quite exciting for me to write a book of such a burning theme- 'justice and love' with reference to rape crime. Although, such crimes take place very regularly here and there in India, it is rather difficult to give a specific picture of rape situation and related laws towards resolution of rape crime cases as they differ according to time and place. It was a great challenge for me to go through the process of writing and to complete this book.

I really thank my teacher, Dr. Shimreingam Shimray (Professor at Eastern Theological College, Jorhat) who spent sleepless nights to format the setting of my book. I do express my deepest gratitude to Dr. R. Vashum (Associate Professor, Sociology Faculty, IGNOU, New Delhi) who took all the trouble to edit and gave the final shape of the book and also for his consent to give foreword to the book. Last of all, I express my gratitude to my wife, Mercy Raman (Jajo) for standing by me in the process of the publication of this book.

It is my sincere belief that the book would be helpful to the readers to comprehend the general contours of addressing rape case and the ways to resolve them. I own responsibility for any discrepancy and weakness of the book.

Jajo Somi

Preface

In view of the general view and attitude in dealing with the cases relating to rape with serious confusion on 'retributive justice' and 'love', this small book intends to examine the nature of relationship between the two for a better understanding of these concepts and their inter-relationships. This piece of work is undertaken with the hypothesis that there is no true love without retributive justice between the rapist and rape victim.

'Retributive justice' is a theory under ethics relating to punishment for crime in one way or the other. The theory cuts across various disciplines such as ethics, law, philosophy, and among others. Generally, the notion is considered as strict as 'tit for tat', but practically it has compensatory component as well. As a result, it serves as an equalizer between the offender and the victim with a view to restoring a just relationship through crime. Besides, it is also a natural law for any crime. In the absence of crime, such law would have no relevance. Its function is to prevent excessive and vengeful punishment, and to deliver justice. By ushering justice, one can see true love for a person as a unique individual. Retributive justice has been variedly viewed by different Christian groups. In some Christian approaches, it is observed that there is priority of love over justice. Many people who are deeply concerned with Christian faith and the centrality of love fail to grasp the meaning of justice. Therefore, it is argued that there can be no possibility to measure justice with a narrow understanding of love, or a misconceived notion of love. In other words, love cannot be lawless. Though distinct, justice and love serve together in times of dealing with crime. Love alone cannot solve the problem of any case, especially the rape case without justice. In this small book, I have attempted to analyze 'retributive justice' and 'love' under the larger framework of 'Christocentric ethics' proposed by Paul Ramsey. This framework is chosen because ethics today, stresses more on duties/responsibilities than on rights, and emphasizes that Christian love be measured through 'worldly justice' in dealing with the case 'similarly' and 'dissimilarly'.

The book mainly focuses on the relationship between 'retributive justice' in the form of 'justice of compensation' and 'love' in the form of 'neighborly love' from Christian perspective with reference to rape victim. The theoretical findings will be based on the decision-making of the case in relation to Indian Penal Code (IPC)

The purpose of this book is to try to overthrow any attempt of decision-making based on strict retributive justice, to elevate obligatory compensation on rapist as a common norm representing justice and love and to decide the case depending on the condition of rape victim and rapist alone. By doing this, it is believed that it will help in formulating the strategy to prevent the incidence of rape in the society.

The book is divided into four chapters. The first chapter deals with the theoretical frames of justice of compensation, neighborly love and Christian love with reference to crime. The second chapter sketches the relationship between justice of compensation and neighborly love under the discourse of Christian love. The third chapter discusses the two different theological approaches that shape the understandings of justice and love in this Christian contemporary world. The fourth chapter is an application of the theoretical findings in the case of rape.

Chapter 1

Defining the Issues

1.1 Introduction

The relationship between retributive justice and ethics of love seems to be insignificant due to the emphasis on the importance of love in this contemporary world. Nevertheless, retributive justice is not totally discounted in any way even as it has a multifaceted meaning. In many countries, it is being practiced to impose repayment at the charge of damage. Here, questions arise: In what basis is this kind of repayment imposed? How can this happen when love works actively in every situation? One can answer these questions that it is due to the vital relations between retributive justice and love. However, many people would still view that repayment is not necessary when the law of love rules the world. In this way, the matter ends up with an endless debate.

On the other hand, one would also encounter the difficulty to grasp the practical meanings of love and forgiveness in the face of confronting different sorts of crime in the contemporary world. It appears that love and forgiveness is a license to commit crime and even to repeat committing crime. Moreover, it seems that love has to be possessed and applied by the victim alone so that the offender can act even at the most heinous nature. By this perspective, one could conclude that love and forgiveness are some kinds of force to victimization when they are regarded without any law of justice. In fact, the truth remains that love cannot be lawless and law cannot be loveless. This truth is also one of the arguments that I have positioned in this book as a matter of discourse.

In the same way, the principle of forgiveness cannot be understood without reasoning and questioning. It would be a sensible approach to extensively apply the principles of justice and love to both the offender and the victim while addressing the issue of crime in the realm of criminal law. This is for the fact that although forgiven, the offender is advised to do something at least toward the victim with the elements of love.

At the backdrop of the hard reality under discussion, I have undertaken to inquire into the relationship between retributive justice and ethics of love under a method called 'Christian love'. For this very purpose, I try to look at them from Christian perspective since retributive justice and love are so dynamically prevalent in Christianity. Under Christian love, I shall discuss retributive justice and ethics of love in the forms of 'justice of compensation', and I shall consider 'neighborly love' as an adequate term in addressing any crime, particularly rape case. Accordingly, in the first chapter, I shall consider how retributive justice is understood as justice of compensation along with its meaning and characteristics.

1.2 Retributive Justice

'Retributive justice' is a theory which is associated with the components of rehabilitation, deterrence and other theories under the ethics of punishment. The theories involve the debate of whether the punishment is regarded as repayment, healing, avoidance, restoration or other elements. Each theory has distinct character in dealing with the issue of punishment. They have certain weaknesses and strengths. Besides, they are ways of interpretation to suit the fitting meaning into the situation of an offending act or in time of committing wrong action in the light of justice.[1]

1.2.1 Meanings of Retributive Justice

The term 'retribution' comes from a word "retribuere", which simply means 'repayment.'[2] It implies the deserved action of giving and taking to someone for an offence in terms of either punishment or reward. However, the meanings understood in worldly and biblical senses are distinct to each other as we shall observe in the following discussion.

1.2.1.1 Worldly Understanding of Retributive Justice

Worldly understanding of retributive justice has four identifiable meanings.

i) Guilt

This is the notion that proves the offender being guilty of breaking the law voluntarily. As a result, retributive justice ensures that the offender deserves to be dealt with legal enforcement for the offence s/he has committed.

ii) Desert

This is the follow up of the notion of guilt. As the person is guilty, punishment has to be meted out exclusively in the sense that it is unjust not to punish the offender. There is no other option of justification. Whether or not the wrongdoer can bear, s/he has to face the consequence for what is done in order to nullify the crime.

---

[1] Stanley Hauerwas, 'Punishing Christians', in *Public Theology for the 21st Century*, edited by William F. Storrar and Andrew R. Morton (New York: T & T Clark, 2004), 287.

[2] 'Retribuere' is a Latin word, in Christopher D. Marshall, *Beyond Retribution: A New Testament Vision for Justice, Crime and Punishment* (Sydney: Lime Grove House Publishing, 2001), 109.

iii) Equivalence

This is the concept commonly considered as proportionality. In finding to be just and fair, the penalty has to be equivalent with the extent of injury. It is after the maxim 'eye for an eye' or 'tit for tat' which must incur penalty but within the limit. It stands as a bulwark for both offender and victim not to gain and lose.

iv) Denunciation

Denunciation has the idea that punishment is a fundamental means by which society should shun and abhor evil acts and set the acceptable standard of behavior. It is a way of avoiding any offence by declaring the guilt and just desert the public. Thus, "Murderers are punished, for example, not simply to reform them or to deter others, but so that they may serve as a powerful witness to the constraints imposed by the moral and legal order."[3]

1.2.1.2 Biblical Understanding of Retributive Justice

In the biblical account, the laws known as 'Decalogue' and other ordinances relating to personal relationship are said to be given as the sign of God's love. In order to retain the relationship between God and the Israelites, the commandments were given to follow in obedience.[4] Most laws are found in the book of Exodus. After Decalogue, the law of retributive justice is attached to violence. Among them, 'eye for eye' is the most visible form of retributive justice resounding the meaning of 'tit for tat'. However, there are variations in its meanings.

i) Natural Law

God gave the 'ten commandments' and other laws to the Israelites as natural laws. The Ten Commandments are known as 'apodictic laws', which are unconditional commanding with the words, 'You shall …'. Besides, other laws concerning human relationship are known as 'casuistic laws', which are conditional commanding with the words,

---

[3] Christopher D. Marshall, 2001, op. cit., 109 ff.

[4] R. Alan Cole, ed., *Exodus: An Introduction and Commentary* (London: InterVarsity Press, 1973), 156.

'If you ....' [5] Casuistic laws are given beyond legal requirements to determine what is due to a person and to his/her fellow from the ethical viewpoint and from the aspect of love. Here, retributive justice is widely known as the law regarding injuries among the casuistic laws.[6]

ii) Criminal Law

Retributive justice is a criminal law in the sense that it judges what the offender has to do to the victim in the crime. In the ordinances, it is informed that any offender should be judged according to the deeds that have been done. There are some examples of restricted crime like, injury with fist or stone, strike with rod, miscarriage, etc., that have to be brought to judgment.[7]

iii) Vengeful Law

Retributive justice reflects the idea of reciprocity and appropriate retaliation rooted in 'lex talionis'. The law spells out 'eye for eye', 'tooth for tooth' *inter alia* indicating that an offender should be punished accordingly. It was given as a means of proper balance in punishing for crimes committed among the Israelites preventing excessive revenge in contrast to the imbalance of punishment practiced in Mesopotamian law.[8]

1.2.2 Evaluation of the Term

There are different meanings of retributive justice based on worldly and biblical understandings. These two approaches do not attach specific image of love tied with the meaning of retributive justice. They emphasize on punishment alone for the committed action in a strict sense as a measure to usher justice and equality. They are limited

---

[5] W. Randolph Tate, *Interpreting the Bible: A Handbook of Terms and Methods* (Massachusetts: Hendrickson Publishers, Inc, 2006), 21.

[6] U. Cassuto's, *A Commentary on the Book of Exodus* (Jerusalem: The Magnes Press, 1967), 263.

[7] R. Alan Cole, ed., 1973, op. cit., 168-169.

[8] Christopher J. H. Wright, *An Eye for an Eye: The Place of Old Testament Ethics Today* (Illinois: InterVarsity Press, 1983), 166.

with a negative sense of punitive reward.[9] However, it is understood that even if the word 'love' was not found in the Decalogue and ordinances, they were given due to covenantal relationship between Yahweh and Israel founded on love.[10] Under this circumstance, many a time compensation replaced retributive justice.

1.2.2.1 Retributive Justice as Justice of Compensation

Despite strict observation of 'tit for tat', the principle of 'equal retribution' in Ancient Near East (ANE) and biblical law, the imposition of fines and imprisonment were also widely practiced with the opinion of rehabilitation and restitution.[11] Retributive justice also reflected much about 'repayment' or the 'charge' for the damage along with punishment theory. On this basis, the term 'justice of compensation' could be appropriately employed for retributive justice to view the contemporary situation. Along with this, the best definition of justice of compensation could be with reference to a concrete action resolved in a flexible way.

i) Moderate Action between Offender and Victim

The prevention of any excessive revenge in obligation of 'eye for eye' reflects the very act of justice and love. This probably enforced people to practice such forms of decision like imprisonment, monetary fines and other alternative forms in those days.[12] They are also being practiced as the best means nowadays in most of the countries. Therefore, it is assumed that the term 'compensation' is relevant to decide any criminal case as a moderate action between victim and offender.

---

[9] Christopher D. Marshall, 2001, op. cit., 109.

[10] Robertson McQuilkin, *An Introduction to Biblical Ethics* (Secunderabad: OM Books, 2002), 4.

[11] George V. Pixley, *On Exodus: A Liberation Perspective* (New York: Orbis Books, 1987), 173-174.

[12] Christopher J. H. Wright, *An Eye for an Eye,* 165-166.

ii) Compromise between Offender and Victim

It is impractical to inflict offender the accurate injury in return. Simultaneously, it is impossible for victim to get the wound restored into an original form. As a result, there is always a search for a means through negotiation. In the process both victim and offender are brought in a mutual agreement by deducting some degree of what they ought to belong and wish. In this very condition, offender is forgiven and victim is compensated in a kenotic (emptying) form.[13] By this, both of them are led to restore the relationship as usual with a mutual exchange of forgiving and compensation.[14]

iii) Similar and Dissimilar Action

From the points of neighborly love, both offender and victim have each responsibility in any situation of crime. Victim must forgive the offender and offender must help the victim in the form of compensation as an ultimate end. Such acts of forgiving and help are the acts of wiping out the penalty towards the offender and the pain with the victim. In doing this, both are at the junction of 'justice-love' that deals with similar and dissimilar aspect of responsibility. Similar aspect means the reciprocal action and dissimilar aspect would mean value aspect.[15]

Therefore, justice of compensation is seen as a holistic approach in which both offender and victim perform their responsibilities because of love and justice. This indicates that in the situation of crime one cannot act with justice without love and vise versa. They are needed equally to bring victim and offender to the meaning of life. In this process, there is no image of loss and gain in between.

---

[13] Philippians (NRSV) 2.

[14] Elizabeth Moberly, *Suffering Innocent and Guilty* (London: SPCK, 1978), 145.

[15] Joseph Thekkinedath, *Love of Neighbour in Mahatma Gandhi* (Bangalore: St. Paul Press Training School, 1973), 164.

1.3 Ethics of Love

Generally, love is considered as the moving force of life. It is defined as the force towards the unity of the divided.[16] Love refers to an inner state of feeling or disposition of heart working through attitude of mind, way of behaving, acting and reacting towards a person and thing. It has a multifaceted meaning understood for different purposes. Therefore, it may be profitable to consider four kinds of love which are rooted in Greek words, viz., 'storge', 'philia', 'eros' and 'agape'. Storge is a familial love or a natural love such as the love of a mother toward a child. Philia is a kind of love such as friendship, brotherly love or neighborly love. Eros is a physical and sensual love such as between husband and wife. Agape is a selfless and unconditional love as the love of God for humankind. This is the love built between God and the people.[17] Even though these four classifications of love are derived from the same source, viz., God, they are all acted through the human heart. Each classification serves and provides certain limited spaces. The relation in the family, community, marriage and in the realm of God retains specific means and end. Hence, agape has been considered under ethics of love for the discussion on neighborly love in this book.

1.3.1 Neighborly Love in the Synoptic Gospels

According to the Bible, the most important teaching of Jesus is the dual commandment - to love God and to love neighbor. It is clear that this teaching was recorded by different writers of the synoptic gospels. They traditionally preserved and interpreted it for teaching and preaching in the church, and finally presented it in the faith document known as the 'Gospel'. Therefore, it is not the teaching taken from understanding with 'Jesus in history' but understanding with 'Jesus in the gospels'. For the writers received, formulated and applied it in a distinct way relevant to the needs of the church during those times. The teaching is limited to Jesus in the gospels alone,

---

[16] Paul Tillich, *Love Power and Justice: Ontological Analysis and Ethical Application* (New York: Oxford University Press, 1954), 25.

[17] 'Love' in *New Dictionary of Theology*, edited by Sinclair B. Ferguson and David F. Wright (Illinois: InterVarsity Press, 1998), 398.

not to Jesus in the universe at large. This indicates that one cannot accept this teaching about love in the gospels to be universal except its concrete relationship with the situation in the history. For it appeared only during the specific time and culture in the gospels and was picked up and used by the evangelists, the writers according to the situation of the people.[18]

Noting the differences, Mark narrated the dual commandment for the purpose of answering the question of a scribe who asked Jesus, 'What is the chief commandment?' Citing the confession of faith in the one God, Jesus replied.[19] Hence, Mark applied the commandment for apologetic purpose. Matthew also made use of the commandment for answering the question of a lawyer among the Pharisees, who tested Jesus by asking, 'teacher, which is the greatest commandment in the law?' Jesus replied with the dual commandment, the first and the second. Hence, Matthew showed that love filled the whole law. Moreover, Luke noted the commandment as the answer from the lawyer to the counter question of Jesus. A lawyer tested Jesus by asking, 'teacher, what shall I do to inherit eternal life?' Subsequently, Jesus asked, 'what do you read in the law?' The lawyer answered, 'love for God and for neighbors'. Thus, Luke narrated the commandment reflecting it as the way to inherit eternal life. Adding to the commandment, Luke narrated the parable of Good Samaritan in order to identify neighbor.[20] These are the differences about the dual commandment in the synoptic gospels. Despite differences, the meanings of neighborly love are synonymous with one another as we shall find in the following discussion.

1.3.1.1 Neighborly Love as Loving God

The dual commandment of Jesus is to love God with the whole being of a person and to love neighbor as self. Being dual, it sounds 'first' and 'second' as mentioned by Matthew. Accordingly, it can also be interpreted into different meanings based on 'more' and 'less'

---

[18] Victor Paul Furnish, *The Love Command in the New Testament* (London: SCM Press Ltd, 1973), 22-23.

[19] There is only One God to be loved, Deuteronomy, 6:4-9.

[20] Victor Paul Furnish, 1973, op. cit., 30-36.

important or 'primary' and 'secondary'. However, in spite of duality, we read it in one meaning without suspicion. There may be many instances that justify the dual love into one and same meaning. It is seen even in the marcan version. In the version, a scribe asked Jesus what the chief commandment was, a common question for the Jews at the time. The questioner wanted to know if the 'chief' was the 'first' of all commandments. Here, Jesus included love for neighbor into love for God in the reply constituting them together into the essence of law that 'there is no other commandment greater than these'. Here, one can argue that the union of the two poles of love makes the complete meaning of the dual love. Otherwise, Jesus might reply with the single love, viz., love for God. In another case, monotheistic culture asserts for people to love God wholeheartedly by observing laws without having any relationship with people. However, Jesus, in his reply turned monotheistic culture into realistic context by adding love for neighbor.[21] This context makes us to understand that loving neighbor is the visible sign of loving God. In other words, the way to love God is to love our fellow beings.

1.3.1.2 Neighborly Love as Concrete Action

In the cultic tradition, love for God was in association with observation of certain laws. On the contrary, Jesus taught that love had fulfilled the whole law. As a result, Matthew testified that all the laws and prophets hang on the dual commandment. By adding love for neighbor, the dual commandment was being visualized into a concrete term. In the gospels of Matthew and Luke, the writers attached traditional materials about loving one's enemies and parable of Good Samaritan to show whom they ought to love. According to Matthew, 'loving the enemy' was considered as the 'higher righteousness' required by a Christian. According to Luke, it was against the hellenistic reciprocity ethic that one should show kindness to those who showed kindness in return. Despite the contradictions, the ability to love enemies draws out the real meaning of dual love.

---

[21] Tom Wright, *Mark for Everyone* (London: Westminster John Knox Press, 2004), 169-172.

For it is not easy to love someone who is against us or whose will manifests no good in return.

It is the attempt to hammer out the real meaning of love in a concrete sense. Moreover, by portraying the Samaritan's service, Jesus symbolizes an effective image of love at work concretely helping a neighbor in time of need.[22] Therefore, giving service and assistance to neighbor has been understood as the obligatory expression of neighborly love.[23]

1.3.1.3 Recognition of Neighbor

The meaning of neighborly love without identifying the neighbor is ambiguous that Jesus incorporates the love of enemy and parable of Good Samaritan in the commandment in Matthew and Luke. Hence, the neighbor is portrayed as enemy and needy in the discourse of loving neighbor.

i) Neighbor as Needy

In contrasting the immediate needy, neighbor is understood as the poor at large. For an example, Jesus drew out the parable of Good Samaritan in order to show the lawyer who neighbor is. In the parable, the Samaritan takes the real figure of Christ and the wounded man, the real figure of neighbor. Through the conversation, the lawyer was forced to assess the description of neighbor and meaning of neighborly love. Thus, the parable show that loving the neighbor means to serve the poor in the concrete terms.[24]

ii) Neighbor as Enemy

In Palestinian Judaism, it was ordinary for the early Christians to bless and pray for enemy to become perfect and righteous as God's people according to Matthew. According to Luke, commandment

---

[22] Eugene LaVerdiere, S.S.S, *Luke: New Testament Message, Volume 5* (Minnesota: The Liturgical Press, 1990), 149-156.

[23] Timothy P. Jackson, *The Priority of Love: Christian Charity and Social Justice* (New Jersey: Princeton University Press, 2003), 12.

[24] Jean Vanier, *Jesus, the Gift of Love* (New York: The Crossroad Publishing Company, 1994), 51.

to love enemy implies the proper interpretation of Jesus' word on non-retaliation. In matthean version, 'enemy' refers to gentiles and to those within Israel itself who opposed the pious. It is also similar to 'those who persecute you', while in the Lucan, to 'those who hate you', who 'curse' and 'abuse you'. The commandment was taken serious because those who obeyed it were ensured to be the "sons of the Most High" as reward. With this expectation the listeners were encouraged to do good to those who could not do good in return.[25]

1.3.2 Love, the Fulfillment of Law and Prophets

Love as the fulfillment of law and prophets is the whole description of Jesus' teaching about both Old and New Testaments of the Bible. In addition, Apostle Paul repeats this notion to the readers of Romans when he writes:

> *'I have come not to abolish but to fulfill'. 'You shall love the Lord your God with all your heart, and with all your soul, and with all your mind'. This is the greatest commandment. And a second is like it: You shall love your neighbor as yourself. On these two commandments hang all the law and the prophets'. In addition, '... love is the fulfillment of the law'.*[26]

Christians have different understandings on these texts and tend to interpret them according to their convenience. Now, the question is how far one can take such interpretations as a guiding force in our daily life. Do they mean that there is no more law of justice at all? If so or not, how shall we justify? The world would be in chaos should the texts really meant to abolish all kinds of law. The texts reflect the termination of law on salvific purpose only but not social laws. Jesus and Paul did not tolerate the Jewish notion of obtaining salvation by observing certain traditions like Sabbath, purification, circumcision, diet, animal sacrifice and alike.[27]

In a strict sense, mosaic laws regulated the whole life and worship of Israel for salvific purpose. In such situation, Jesus as the

---

[25] Eugene LaVerdiere, S.S.S, 1990, op. cit., 94-97.

[26] Matthew 5:17, 22:37 - 40 and Romans 13:10 (NRSV).

[27] Herbert McCabe, *What is Ethics all About?* (Washington: Corpus Publication, 1969), 6-7.

son of God justified his lordship on Sabbath and authority over Moses and later prophets. Consequently, Jesus summed up the mosaic statutes into two – love for God and love for neighbor as the core in one's life. Thus, it was a right time for Jesus to say that he came to fulfill the law given through prophets beginning with Moses, but not to abolish them. In the same way, Paul did defend Jesus' work of atonement. Unless Jesus died on the cross, the Jewish religious laws and practices could have been valid to a great extent. However, since Jesus had already atoned for humankind, it was not necessary to keep such laws.

Paul also argued that circumcision was not necessary for gentiles to become the people of God. He was also convinced of the importance of social relationship that can be built up by neighborly love. Hence, Paul also pronounced that 'love fulfills the law.'[28] However, by such pronouncement of 'fulfillment', it does not mean that love has eradicated all the social laws. This was how Jesus commanded the Pharisees to obey Roman emperor by giving tax, which set example for all governments in the world. Similarly, Paul urged the readers to be subject to the governing authorities by giving taxes and revenue because they were instituted by God. Besides, he also acknowledged the use of sword of the authorities with a purpose. This would mean that the subjects have to obey the higher authorities; otherwise it is right for them to judge them even with sword.[29]

1.4 "Christian Love"

The kind of Christian ethics introduced by Paul Ramsey is thoroughly 'Christocentric'[30] and deontological in nature.[31] Under this ethics, he proposed Christian love as an approach in his ethical framework

---

[28] See 'Law in New Testament', in *Dictionary of the Bible,* edited by James Hastings, sixth printing (New York: Hendrickson Publishers, Inc., 2005), 535-537.

[29] Matthew 22:21 and Romans 13:1-7 (NRSV).

[30] Roger H. Crook, *Introduction to Christian Ethics* (New Jersey: Prentice Hall, 2002), 34.

[31] Paul Ramsey, *Basic Christian Ethics* (London: SCM Press Ltd, 1950), 166.

during his stay at Princeton University in1950.[32] This approach was proposed based on his understanding of the relationship between the Bible and Christian ethics. To him, the Bible is redacted into a norm by 'Christian love' through self-inverted love as the universal truth. This principle is more or less taken from the core of Jesus' teaching about neighborly love in the gospels.[33] Thus, he consents that every social policy should be sorted out according to Jesus' teaching of love. In trying to build up the relation between justice of compensation and neighborly love, I have applied Christian love as a workable basis. The reasons for the assumptions are -

(a) Christian love never ceases to deal with social policy in a dissimilar way.
(b) It pursues to decide any issue from neighbor's perspective.
(c) It stresses that every issue has to be sorted out through disinterested love.
(b) Christian love is universalized as a mandate beyond the gospels.

These points are very significant even though the writer does not explicitly convince the readers. Relating to this, Ramsey precisely claims that Christian ethics has to shift from rights to responsibilities.[34] This ethical frame tends to depart from biblical norms to worldly norms in a general sense. Moreover, his notion of Christian love as a universal validity for moral code proves the relation between the Bible and Christian ethics. By the principle of Christian love, he draws the standard of Christian ethics from self-inverted love in a person. Therefore, he says, "a Christian man lives not in himself but in Christ and his neighbor. Otherwise, he is not a Christian."[35] With such understanding, we can now briefly discuss on the related subject matter as the following.

---

[32] It is his own hand writing in the introductory part of his book, "Basic Christian Ethics".

[33] Paul Ramsey, *Deeds and Rules in Christian Ethics:* Scottish Journal of Theology Occasional Paper No.11 (London: Oliver and Boyd, 1967), 26.

[34] Paul Ramsey, 1950, op. cit., 354.

[35] Paul Ramsey, 1950, op. cit., 100-101.

1.4.1 Sources of Christian Love

The origin of Christian love is rooted in two sources. The first is the righteousness of God, which is essentially the same as 'justice'. Righteousness is rooted in the very nature of God while dealing with people through the redemptive work of Jesus. The second is the kingdom of God in which the teaching of Jesus prevails. Jesus' teaching is not as a means to solve the human issues and to bring people to the kingdom, but it is as itself in decision-making without conforming to situation in any form.[36]

1.4.2 Meaning of Christian Love

Its primary meaning always reflects disinterested love based on 'love your neighbor'. For disinterested love never seeks one's own good, but the good of one's neighbor.[37] It is bound by a duty rather than right towards one's neighbor in a concrete sense. Here, though inseparable, duty is more accountable than right because duty is need-based of an individual, whereas, right is value-based of society in the constitution.[38] Therefore, Christian love seeks to decide whom the duty has to be rendered among the people as a concrete help. Even though everybody is ought to be loved equally, since one cannot do good to everybody, Christian love refers its concern to those who falls in need. This shows that Christian ethics means "neighbor-centered concern for value" at the expense of one's own self. Under this circumstance, it is understood that Christian love generates dissimilar decision of policymaking through disinterested love based on need.[39]

---

[36] Roger H. Crook, 2002, op. cit., 34-35.

[37] Gene H. Outka, 'Character, Conduct and the Love Commandment', in *Norm and Context in Christian Ethics,* edited by Gene H. Outka and Paul Ramsey (London: SCM Press Ltd, 1969), 41.

[38] Jose Kuttianimattathil, SDB, *Theological Anthropology: A Christian Vision of Human Beings* (New Delhi: Rekha Printers Pvt. Ltd, 2009), 271-272.

[39] Paul Ramsey, 1950, op. cit., 157 ff.

1.4.3 Christian Love as Universal Mandatory

Being normative under deontological nature, Ramsey's ethics is believed to seek obligation as the ultimate goal in the realm of moral judgment of right and wrong.[40] Therefore, he stressed Christian love rooted in unaffected God's righteousness and kingdom of God as the first point. Second, he stressed the fulfillment of law by love for God and love for the neighbor. Third, he dragged it into the social policy to be the decisive force. No matter of size and form, it is convinced that Christian love should be dominant and free in the decision-making. In such principle, Christian love is set as the universal mandate for ethical norm in every situation. Moreover, this is coined to be the sovereign rule of life carried out as duty based on need of the neighbor.[41]

1.4.4 Christian Love into Social Policy

In this contemporary world, there is an attempt to relate the Bible and Christian ethics both in theory and in practice.[42] Under this circumstance, it is true to let Christian love search for social policy without conforming to it by nature. It has to sink into the best possible actions or norms remaining free and dominant in any partnership and context. For it is said, "it does not transform itself into the coin of any realm, though it enters in every realm and becomes debtor both to the Greek and to the barbarians."[43] Besides, Christian love never treats any case similarly. It therefore means "treating similar cases dissimilarly, regarding the good of any other individual as more than our own when he and you alone are

---

[40] James Walter Gustafson with Joseph B. Onyango-Okello, *The Quest for Truth: An Introduction to Philosophy* (Massachusetts: Proclaim Publication, 2007), 143-144.

[41] For details, refer 'Introduction', in *Christian Ethics: An Introductory Reader,* edited by Hunter Mabry (Delhi: ISPCK, 2002), 13-14.

[42] Bruce C. Birch and Larry L. Rasmussen, 'Relating the Bible and Christian Ethics: Recent Efforts' in *Christian Ethics: An Introductory Reader,* edited by Hunter P. Mabry, 121.

[43] Paul Ramsey, 1950, op. cit., 344.

involved."[44] It creates community by attributing value to persons and preserves community by working through power systems for justice.[45] In such a case, Christian love is adopted to decide how and in what way justice should be worked out in balance.

1.5 Conclusion

Justice of compensation and neighborly love are both distinct in nature. Nevertheless, they are inseparable whichever and whenever the issue arises in the society. Without justice of compensation, there is no point of neighborly love, and without neighborly love, there is no point of concrete action during the crime. Within them, Christian love works effectively in order to make a visible relationship between them. In the process, the work of Christian love 'in a dissimilar way' helps compensation to be a flexible form on the one hand. On the other hand, the work of Christian love in disinterested love helps neighborly love to be self-dedicated. Under this stance, the society is directed to identify the need, neighbor and the concrete action in an approachable way. Therefore, both victim and offender can be brought into a considerable judgment without bias in any crime, particularly in a rape case. In this situation, both actions of forgiveness and compensation are worked out without the notion about punishment and injury. Damage is replaced by compensation and revenge by forgiveness. The roles of justice of compensation, neighborly love and Christian ethics are characteristic and inseparable in every possible way.

---

[44] Paul Ramsey, 1950, op. cit., 234.

[45] Roger H. Crook, 2002, op. cit., 35.

Chapter 2

The Place and Role of Christian Love

2.1 Introduction

It is generally considered that the synoptic Gospels were written in the specific time and culture of Jewish nation during Jesus. Besides, the writers wrote them according to different purposes in their own time. In this circumstance, the dual commandment was also attached for the specific reasons in the way the writers tried to convince people of that time. None of the writers intended that the commandment should be for universal validity. The commandment was just attributed to those who came to Jesus whether to test him or to question him about inheritance of the kingdom of God. In such situation, Jesus answered by love in the way that they should follow. One of the most striking notes was the fulfillment of law and prophets by love, as Matthew stated. His conception of the law and the prophets was also so expressed in the Golden Rule, 'for this is the law and the prophets.'[46]

[46] Victor Paul Furnish, 1973, op. cit., 32.

Now, to what extent can the conceptions of Matthew about law and the prophets be based on literally? It is the task of the readers to meticulously understand his conception in order to avoid confusion. In other words, the context needs to be properly understood. Otherwise, one may be led to misinterpret his concept as meaning the appropriation for elimination of all laws of justice. Besides, it would be dangerous to mean that there is no question about justice while the term 'meeting the need' is so factual. It will also be over simplistic to say that love is the answer for everything. Unfortunately, the exaggeration of love over justice has really touched the very heart of Christian preaching in many places.

Hence, it is required to build the necessary relationship between justice of compensation and neighborly love without any prejudice. The relationship is especially preferred to the situation of victims and offenders in any crime. Without crime, the relationship can be ineffective as much as possible at any time. Here, Christian love plays a central role of bringing them together as they play their own roles of bringing victims and offenders together. By such attempts, it is possible for justice of compensation and neighborly love to bring both offender and victim together to a considerable and satisfactory solution in any issue.[47]

2.2 The Roles of Justice of Compensation, Neighborly Love and Christian Love

Justice of compensation, neighborly love and Christian love are holistic purpose for social issue. Like a three-face object, they appear and work together for the same purpose. There is no question about more importance and less importance among the faces. In case, one face among them fails the whole object disfigures and renders worthless. They play their specific own roles that make the object vital by supplementing and involving with one another. Therefore, it will be relevant to point out their roles specifically lest they are ambiguous and indefinite.

[47] http://en.wikipedia.org/restorativejustice (12 December 2010).

2.2.1 Justice of Compensation in Concrete Action

There are different conceptions of justice like, 'similar treatment for a similar case', 'to each according to merits and works' and 'to each according to needs'. Here, justice of compensation falls on the last category. This kind of justice always tries to see the condition of the person's need whether big or small and similar or dissimilar.[48] According to the need, it works to execute in a concrete term without fail. In failing this, the love of a person for his /her neighbor tends to be unreal and emotional. Besides, the commandment of Jesus to love one's neighbor will be ineffective and even invalid too when someone's need whether in a crime or other is ignored. To be sure, 'love your neighbor' reflects the concrete action towards a person who is in the condition of sickness, nakedness, hunger, injury and so on. Such is the situation that disinterested love is believed to implement without any bias of any form. Therefore, one can certainly say that concrete action justifies the act of a person's love for other. By such action only especially through crime, it is acknowledged that justice of compensation really attains the true meaning of love.[49]

2.2.2 Neighborly Love towards Neighbor

The concept of 'neighbor' is crucial to the Christians as emphasized in the commandment to love someone's neighbor. This commandment shows who our neighbor is and what it means. The term 'neighbor' is the location from where we can begin with two philosophical concepts. First, the commandment to love one's neighbor is a test of God. Biblically God wants us to love Him with our total being. In order to fulfill this, we are commanded to love our neighbors as a necessary test. By doing so, we are going to be counted as the one who love God. By failing it, we are going to be counted as the one who do not love God. As a result, it says, "if a man say, I love God and hateth his brother, he is a liar". Besides, the commandment reflects the affirmation of our belief in God. Loving the neighbor

---

[48] Gene Outka, *Agape: An Ethical Analysis* (Massachusetts: Alpine Press, 1972), 91-92.

[49] Albrecht Ritschl, *Three Essays,* translated by Philip Hefner (Philadelphia: Fortress Press, 1972), 253.

speaks how we know and believe God. As a result, it is claimed that such love exhausts the material content of agape.[50] Therefore, it is concluded that the role of neighborly love expresses the essence of horizontal and vertical relationships.

2.2.3 Christian Love in Decision Making

It has been discussed that Christian love always searches for social policy to determine a proper social ethic. Thus, it indicates to work out the absolute demands of God in the social realm. Being free and dominant, it is never communed with any other social ethics. However, it penetrates the social issue to solve realistically as yeas in the dough. It does not precede any law or existing conventions of society but directs them to meeting neighbor's need in a concrete term.[51] Negating the 'natural law', love is presupposed to be the decisive factor in favor of the need arising. Irrespective of the size and value, any issue has to take into account a considerable settlement by adjustment. It tries to deal with even similar case in a dissimilarly way according to the condition of a person. Therefore, to quote Ramsey (1950:338), "Christian love formulates social policy by taking into account every concrete element in the situation which determines how in fact some actual good may be done for the neighbor in the state of civil society and the relationships among people existing at present."[52] Under this circumstance, we are called to build up our moral responsibility towards the neighbor through disinterested love.

2.3 The Midpoint between Justice of Compensation and Neighborly Love

Christian love plays a significant role as the midpoint in the relationship between justice of compensation and neighborly love. This midpoint dictates justice of compensation and neighborly love to appear equally in terms of both quality and quantity. The relationship can be drawn from two levels, i.e., theoretical and practical points of view.

---

[50] Gene Outka, 1972, op. cit., 44-46.

[51] Paul Ramsey, 'The Case of the Curious Exception', in *Norm and Context in Christian Ethics,* edited by Gene H. Outka and Paul Ramsey (1969), 91.

[52] Paul Ramsey, 1950, op. cit., 338-341.

2.3.1 Relation from Theoretical Point of View

The theoretical point of view on the relationship between justice of compensation and neighborly love is based on mutual and complimentary characteristics. Mutual characteristic deals with the conditions of 'damage' under justice of compensation and 'need' under neighborly love, and the complimentary deals with the balance between spiritual and physical aspects that depend on each other.

2.3.1.1 Mutual Relationship

Mutual relationship has to do with interdependency and interconnection between any individual and any party, without which an individual and a party cannot work in a full swing for one particular purpose. In such case, justice of compensation and neighborly love cannot perform their roles fully for a particular purpose without having mutual relationship between them. Being dependent and interconnected, justice of compensation and neighborly love serve for two parties in the best possible way.[53]

i) Compensation along with Damage

Of course, there may be various forms of hurt in the crime but every hurt is a serious matter because it changes the whole lifestyle of victim instantly even affecting the lifestyle of offender to some extent. It can be small or little both qualitatively and quantitatively, the matter of hurt may evolve to a big crime conditionally. The conditions depend on the intentional and unintentional causes of damage and on the approaches of dealing with the matter in the crime. Hence, the conditions have to be examined thoroughly till the whole arena of the crime is perceptible. After which the responsibilities of both victim and offender can be worked out to heal them physically, mentally and spiritually. Here, some people may come for a help with the image of restoration but such help will only heal the physical wound leaving mental and spiritual wounds behind, which are more serious

[53] For elaborate discussion on the mutual relationship between justice of compensation and neighborly love, refer 'Covenant', in *New Dictionary of Theology*, 173.

than physical dimension in one way.[54] Since it is the case, only offender-compensation matters here as a norm to restore the image of physical, mental and spiritual damages. It is as the unavoidable system of justice at any time and cost till crime remains as usual in the society.[55]

ii) Neighborly Love along with Need

The term 'need' is a very pathetic but very powerful in the sense that it attracts outsiders to help in terms of material, psychological, physical and spiritual. It is caused under certain reasons either by force or by weakness. Here, hurt in a crime is considered as the point of need from the angle of neighborly love, and its cause is calculated as by force. Hurt exhibits need because it is embodied with weakness, defame and distress in physical, mental and spiritual aspects. Therefore, neighborly love never overlooks such condition by nature because it comes into effect by an ethics of fulfilling need alone out of the bondage of deficiency. This ethics implicitly is rooted in the Nazareth Manifesto where Jesus states about good news to the poor, release to the captives, recovery sight to the blind and delivery of the oppressed. On this basis, hurt in the crime is remedial without any condition.[56]

2.3.1.2 Complimentary Relationship

According to Agapic nature of love, we are bound to love God and love one another without any condition. This kind of enforcement is rooted in His unconditional love towards the whole world. Human love towards God and every created being and thing is subjected to God's inclusive love.[57] Hence, horizontal love is very effective to realize

---

[54] Stanley J. Rowland, Jr, *Ethics, Crime and Redemption: Christian Perspectives on Social Problems* (Philadelphia: The Westminster Press, n.d.), 76.

[55] 'Mastership; the Divine Law', in http://www.denverspiritualcommunity.org/Wisdom/Mastership5htm (December 17, 2010).

[56] Canon Leon Morris, *Luke: An Introduction and Commentary,* revised edition (Michigan: InterVarsity Press, 2000), 116-117.

[57] C.W. Christian, *Friedrich Schleiermacher,* edited by Bob E. Patterson (Texas: Word Books Publisher, 1979), 137.

vertical love in a general sense. In such case, horizontal love becomes more consequential in a particular situation of crime by exercising the principle of justice of compensation and neighborly love without which vertical love merges into unrealistic and mythological nature.

i) No Neighborly Love without Justice of Compensation

There is no question of how much a person should exercise the principles of justice of compensation and neighborly love in the situation of crime. They appear as an ultimate norm in order to achieve wellbeing in both physical and spiritual aspects. From the physical point of view, the principles express the help of the needy in the society, and from the spiritual point of view, the principles signify the worship of God. For it is understood, "one cannot love the heavenly Father without loving Christ, and one cannot love Christ without loving his neighbor."[58] In these circumstances, how can one say that s/he loves and worships God without caring of those who are in need? It is impossible to build up vertical relationship by ignoring horizontal relationship according to the Agapic nature of love. Therefore, in case a person has no spirit of helping the needy, s/he as offender, fails to help victim in crime and fails loving and worshipping God as well.[59]

ii) No Justice of Compensation without Neighborly Love

To Mahatma Gandhi, it is impossible for a person to obtain self-realization in this life without the service to one's neighbor. Besides, he admits, "the immediate service of all human beings becomes a necessary part of the endeavor simply because the only way to find God is to see Him in His creation and be one with it. This can only be done by service of all."[60] Similarly, it is impossible for a person to become Christian in her or his life without loving the neighbors. For a person who does not apply love for wellbeing, will only render to individualize and sentimentalize love. In such case, if a victim cannot forgive offender, what is the point for the victim to love

---

[58] Joseph Thekkinedath, 1973, op. cit., 190.

[59] I John 4:20 (NRSV).

[60] Joseph Thekkinedath, 1973, op. cit., 164 & 187.

her or his enemy? It is clear that for a victim, forgiving offender is the sign of loving and worshipping God in the true sense. In case forgiveness[61] is unnoticed in a complimentary design with the offender-compensation, definitely the matter of compensation ceases superfluously in any crime.[62]

2.3.2 Relation from Practical Point of View

Christian love plays a decisive role between justice of compensation and neighborly love to be exercised in the context of crime. Therefore, as noted earlier, it has become the mid-point that determines how victim and offender want to be. Moreover, it guides them to do good till the meeting point of the contesting opinions is arrived at. To be true, without Christian love, an act of neighborly love may nullify justice on the one hand, and on the other, the act of justice may supersede love with the pressure of retribution. Therefore, when they are expected to go together, both victim and offender are safe and free from the consequence of crime. Being victim, s/he is enabled to feel free from the loss and being offender, from the guilt for damage.

2.3.2.1 Justice of Compensation under Christian Love

Justice of compensation mostly reflects the solution of any crime. Consequently, it exhibits the rights of both victim and offender - the rights to 'give and take' as statute. Victim is always in the position to receive what is due at the charge of the damage, and offender is always in the position to pay back accordingly. These are the rights to be worked out under an agreement between victim and offender through negotiation. The execution of the rights is the sign of compromise that shows there is no more debt between them.[63] Of course, forgiveness and compensation are not related to each other, but they are under 'right to give' and 'right to receive.'[64] They have to

[61] Forgiveness is as a kind of help in order to heal an offender from the perspective of justice of compensation and neighborly love.

[62] Gene Outka, 1972, op. cit., 86.

[63] Christopher D. Marshall, 2001, op. cit., 132.

[64] There is no such condition 'not to forgive' in the absence of compensation. Moreover, there is also no such condition to forgive in the absence of compensation

follow crime even though they do not follow each other. Forgiveness is the will of God from the perspective of violence, and compensation is the will of God from the perspective of justice. By the value of justice, offender restitutes in the form of compensation, and by the cost of love; victim forgives and accepts compensation. What both victim and offender want to do to each other is done consecutively. This is the solution of crime in the light of love by breaking all barriers and disintegrations. Thus, the actions of both forgiveness and compensation fulfill the ethics of justice of compensation and neighborly love.[65]

2.3.2.2 Neighborly Love under Christian Love

It is remarkable to say that the true meaning of love lies in the situation of crime. As a result, the understanding of neighborly love for the needy and the enemy will be vague without discussing it in such situation. Here, the word 'needy' depicts the reality of victim and the word 'enemy', the reality of offender in any crime. Now the important question is how they respond to each other according to their own convictions at the heart of crime. In fact, from the perspective of love, both of them are victims of different shapes that need help. In such situation, there remains nothing to be practiced except love as norm in different forms. Therefore, being in unusual status, both victim and offender are required to practice the principle of love through different levels in order to overcome the consequence of crime. Otherwise, they will remain in a miserable and crippled life.[66]

i) Position of Victim

Victim is always in the position of defeat, defame, weakness and alike physically, psychologically and spiritually. Even if so, s/he has to look at the condition of offender with the helping spirit and to find out what offender needs most by the power of neighborly love. Offender is also considered here to be a kind of victim because of the evil action by which s/he is psychologically depressed in return. Here,

---

and vice versa.

[65] Herbert McCabe, 1969, op. cit., 5.

[66] Stanley J. Rowland, Jr, n.d. op. cit., 84.

it is clear that forgiveness is the only means to deliver her or him from this stage. As knowing this, victim has the courage to forgive offender so that s/he resumes the normal life. In this situation, victim is the only right person to forgive. No one who comes to console offender for the evil act cannot affect the act of forgiveness, which should be carried out by victim alone.[67]

ii) Position of Offender or Enemy

By no means, offender can overlook love assuming as if only victim can practice. S/he should re-examine how far neighborly love facilitates them to help one another in the situation created by crime. Then, offender is led to reflect why not to help victim if victim can forgive. With this understanding, the way to restitute the damage in the form of compensation has become a help towards needy. This act of compensation has become an unavoidable for offender in the case of crime, and s/he is the only right person to carry out this act. Even if there is any monetary compensation from government or non-governmental organizations (NGOs), such act cannot replace the act of compensation that has to be carried out by offender alone.[68]

From this perspective of neighborly love, both victim and offender are carrying the image of victim in different categories through which they are supposed to help one another without fail. They are bound by love that both of them have to practice in order to rebuild their disordered life to normalcy. Here, forgiveness and compensation are the only norms to help one another in the situation of crime because solution is the only objective that is expected between them. Being victim and offender, they exclusively expect such counsels about help towards needy more than any other good news. However, helps that come from other sources cannot affect the act of forgiveness and compensation of their own. For the solution to crime is required only within them.[69]

---

[67] T.W. Manson, *Ethics and the Gospel* (New York: SCM Press Ltd., 1960), 64.

[68] For further clarity, see 'Crimes and Punishments', in *Dictionary of the Bible,* 167.

[69] http://www.direct.gov.uk/enCrimeJusticeAndTheLaw/VictimsOfCrime/DG_177421 (17 December 2010).

2.3.2.3. Neighbors in the Situation of Crime

There is a human tendency to face difficulty of having mutual relationship between victim and offender. However, Christian love never permits this situation of difficulty in any case due to the same image in which human beings are created. Even if we get angry, we are reminded not to be angry till evening,[70] and are supposed to live by forgiveness. In such condition, it is difficult for the Christians to pronounce even such language of 'victim' or 'offender' by the power of love. Therefore, it is important for the victim and the offender to have a firm conviction to accept one another as neighbors in love that breaks all such barriers and enmities. In the situation of crime, both of them definitely require justice and love simultaneously through which any difficulty can be discussed to work out solution. Here, neighborly love is the most significant kind of love that they should ever expect when they are to be helped as needy.[71]

i) Victim as the Neighbor of Offender

We often hear about conflict that divides people – the side of victim on the one hand and the side of offender on the other. As a result, it is usual to build up hatred, enmity, maladjustment, etc., beyond love. However, the term 'neighbor' is a very meaningful and effective term in biblical understanding. At the most, it is the term to help one another when people are in need or in trouble. From this perspective, offender is not supposed to walk away forgetting the violent act done. S/he has to look back instantly to the person whom s/he has hurt keeping in mind the status of being a victim and the role of neighborly love. At the very moment of harm, the wounded person becomes victim, and thus, offender becomes the right person to help victim according to justice of compensation and neighborly love. Moreover, victim is no more a kind of person other than the closest neighbor of offender. Therefore, by the help of offender towards victim, both are saved to the normal life as it is

---

[70] Ephesians 4:26.

[71] Karl Barth, *The Epistle to the Romans,* sixth ed., translated by Edwyn C. Hoskyns (London: Oxford University Press, 1933), 452.

in the most possible way.[72] By doing this, offender is counted as a righteous person both in the eyes of God and people. Moreover, this act of help towards victim is the means for offender to reconcile with God and the 'other', and is the expression of worship to God.[73]

ii) Offender or Enemy as the Neighbor of Victim

It happens even if physical wound is healed mental wound remains. Therefore, forgiveness cannot be one-sided. To show the complete meaning of forgiveness, victim has to forgive offender both in the flesh and mind. Forgiveness is a matter of honesty - 'speaking the truth in love', which implies 'no vengeance' despite expressing the feeling of pain.[74] At this juncture the offender is expected to show a benevolent act towards victim for the deed of pain caused by certain act. This is how the role of justice and love attempt to resolve the problem in a crime. Even though both victim and offender suffer from different angles, they are not discouraged to act out forgiveness and compensation by the notion of 'meeting the need' or the term of 'neighbor'. To say, victim suffers from pain caused with the evil and offender suffers from impending results of the deed. In such situation, as soon as the act of forgiveness and compensation is carried out in the way to help one another as neighbor, the dilemma of the crime is instantly dissolved with the nominal scars of pain and shame. By such approach, both victim and offender can see the true meaning of love that unites and builds people in harmony.[75]

2.3.3 Humility in the Situation of Crime

It does not disappoint us to admit that moral law reflects on humility too according to the personal conviction. As a result, it is our ethical task to reflect humility in the attempt of decision-making. Regarding

---

[72] It is mentioned in the introductory part of the 'Victim–offender Reconciliation Programs John Howard Society of Alberta, 1998, retrieved from http://www.johnhoward.ab.ca/pub/pdf/c27.pdf (December 12, 2010).

[73] Miriam Perlewitz, M.M., *The Gospel of Matthew* (Wilmington: Michael Glazier Inc., 1988), 66.

[74] Christopher D. Marshall, 2001, op. cit., 272-273.

[75] Roger H. Crook, 2002, op. cit., 89.

humility, Paul exhorted the readers in Philippi as "let each of you look not to your own interests, but to the interests of others."[76] This scenario is also seen in the Sermon of Mount about retaliation.[77] On the contrary to the law of retribution, it exposes that one should not resist an evildoer followed by offering another cheek, giving additional cloth, adding another mile to go and accepting someone's beg. Of course, the literal meaning of the text may be impractical from the point of violence that propagates the denial of one's life or liberty.[78] For no one is advised to welcome the one who comes seeking an opportunity to destroy. However, the text reveals the truth of accepting the one who comes seeking to fulfill her /his interest in term of need whatsoever physically, psychologically and spiritually.

In the situation of crime, being defected persons in different forms as noted above, both victim and offender raise their interests to be fulfilled by one another. They need each other as the right persons in order to remove traumas from them. Here, victim wishes if offender pays something for the damage and offender wishes, if victim forgives for the same. By this, they want each other to fulfill their own interests in term of help.[79] From the side of victim, compensation represents as help to heal the wound, and from the side of offender, forgiveness represents as help to eradicate the impending consequence. Under this circumstance, the acts of justice of compensation and neighborly love meet the need of humility in the situation of crime. What offender wants victim to do for her or him is done in the form of forgiveness and what victim wants offender to do for her or him is done in the form of compensation in an equal method.[80] Also being neighbors, they help one another in order to overcome the feature of crime. Hostility is not expected between them as far as the services of justice of compensation and

---

[76] Philippians 2:4 (NRSV).

[77] Matthew 5:38-42 (NRSV).

[78] Robert Bruch McLaren, *Christian Ethics: Foundations and Practice* (New Jersey: Prentice Hall, 1994), 226-227.

[79] Justice always reflects the satisfaction of others, in Jeffrey Reiman, *Justice and Modern Moral Philosophy* (London: Yale University Press, 1990), 211.

[80] Christ Wood, *The End of Punishment: Christian Perspective on the Crisis in Criminal Justice* (Edinburgh: Saint Andrew Press, 1991), 10.

neighborly love work with humility. In fact, they are more than norm. They are a matter of humility in one's lifetime. As long as they are active in the social programs, the search for God's intervention arises in the same time.[81]

2.4 Conclusion

Despite differences of role, justice of compensation, neighborly love and Christian love work for one intrinsic purpose. Theoretically, the activity of Christian love always guides the activities of justice of compensation and neighborly love side by side till it reaches the point of solution. To be realistic, Christian love stands as fortification between them so that they grant the criminal case to be soluble. Moreover, it strengthens them to build both horizontal and vertical relationships in balance. As a result, justice of compensation and neighborly love cannot separate each other at all. The relationship is shaped by mutual and complimentary standpoints. By this, their results balance horizontal and vertical relationships as the main goal simultaneously. In order to achieve this goal, both victim and offender are expected to accept and help one another breaking all barriers of enmity between them under the principle of give and take. Here, being victim, s/he is supposed to forgive the offender and being offender, to help victim in the form of compensation. By doing this, both victim and offender are saved from the clutch of crime and feeling of 'loss and gain', and are enabled to resume their normal life without any condition. At the most, justice of compensation and neighborly love convey that both victim and offender love and worship God in their own way by accomplishing their own tasks of help towards one another through the experience of crime. Apparently, forgiveness is what offender wishes victim to do and compensation is what victim wishes offender to do for the same reason viz., evil deed upon victim.

---

[81] Miriam Perlewitz, M.M., 1988, op. cit., 34-35.

Chapter 3

The Function of Justice of Compensation

3.1 Introduction

People have different views about love and justice in this contemporary world. Reflecting the dual commandment, many Christians tend to interpret love as the most powerful criterion without the question of justice. Therefore, it seems that 'love over justice' becomes the Christian standard every now and then. By love as the fulfillment of law, many have negated the faces of justice in every situation. Here, I believe that this overemphasis of love over justice is due to the different conceptions of authority of the Bible. People speak about the authority of the Bible based on literal reading such as mentioned, "... until heaven and earth pass away, not one letter, not one stroke of a letter, will pass from the law..." and "all scripture is inspired by God... ."[82] It is so provoking that some churches are influencing

[82] Matthew 5:18 and 2 Timothy 3:13 (NRSV) are the examples assumed to read in a literal sense.

the mass of Christians and others as well to live a life suiting the literal meaning of the Bible. Consequently, people tend to assume the words, 'forgive' and 'forget' as the very heart of neighborly love in crime. There is no doubt about forgiving by the power of love. However, forgiveness has become unconditional for them. Besides, by this kind of teaching, the meaning of the law of justice has been totally deviated and driven away from the very practical sense of life. Such misconception and narrow understanding about love and justice could be dangerous. However, it must be kept in mind that no person or group of people is/are to be blamed for this development in the society. The development has come due to the hermeneutic standard basing on the two schools of theology namely, the Alexandrian and Antiochene theologies that have been coming down as the offshoot of Christian schools of thought from the past.

Therefore, this chapter shall focus on the influence of these two schools of theology that has been shaping the life of people with reference to their contributions to the relationship between justice of compensation and neighborly love. The discussion shall enable us to understand what justice of compensation actually means in the light of love wiping out all the negative senses like, compensation as punishment and revenge. In the process, s/he can then freely choose whether to apply or to hamper compensation in the time of crime, especially rape case.

3.2 Christian Schools of Thought

Christian schools of thought are rooted in twin biblical truths of the divine transcendence and the divine immanence. The divine transcendence stresses that God is self-sufficient existing above and apart from the universe but relates the world as Transcendent One from beyond, basing on the Scripture like in the Hebrew as "God is in Heaven and you are on earth". Whereas, the divine immanence stresses that God is active within the universe and is involved with the process of the world and of human history as Immanent One, basing on the presence of God's Spirit as sustainer of creation, Jesus' acclamations that credited natural processes like, the beauty of flowers to the agency of Father and alike.[83] Within these truths, two Christian schools of theology namely, Alexandrian and Antiochene theologies follow the similar tracks of belief system in the understanding of the person of Jesus Christ.[84] Consequently, this difference may be one of the factors to brand the names of theological approach such as 'classical' and 'modern approaches'. By and large, classical approach follows Antiochene base and modern approach falls along the Alexandrian base. Despite differences, three groups - fundamental, orthodox and evangelical are under the category of 'classical approach' because of their stands on Antiochene understanding. On the contrary, modern approach arose based on Alexandrian understanding in modern century.[85] This has been the ground of classical and modern approaches to be in contest in this contemporary world. Therefore, I am trying to discuss up to what extent these two approaches influence the understanding of justice of compensation and neighborly love in order to help liberating people from the governance of narrow biblicism.[86]

3.2.1 The Basis of Classical Approach

In fact, there may be various internal differences between fundamentalist, orthodox and evangelical schools of thought. However, they are almost the same due to their positions on transcendental stream. This may be one of the reasons that they fall together into one category viz., classical approach, which holds onto the Antiochene theological basis, 'from above'. Standing on this, the understanding about God and the universe is never reconciled with human experience and reason but is received in obedience from

[83] Cf. 'Introduction: Transcendence and Immanence and Modern theological History', in *20th Century Theology: God and the World in a Transitional Age*, edited by Stanley J. Grenz and Roger E. Olson (Secunderabad: OM Books, 2004), 11.

[84] Kuncheria Pathil and Dominic Veliath, *An Introduction to Theology: Indian Theological Series* (New Delhi: Rekha Printers Pvt. Ltd., 2003), 94.

[85] The editors of *20th Century Theology: God and the World in a Transitional Age* elaborately discussed about the mentioned schools of thought based on 'from above' and 'from below' clubbed into 'classical approach' and 'liberal approach' under Transcendence and Immanence.

[86] C.W. Christian, 1979, op. cit., 131.

God's revelation.[87] For better understanding of this approach, we shall acquaint with some of the important mainstreams that can be considered as the backbone of classical approach.

3.2.1.1 Authority of the Scripture

The Bible is the scripture of Christians. It is the greatest source about God and the universe that Christians ever receive without any hesitation. There is no problem in the accumulation of knowledge from the Bible. However, the emphasis of the authority of the Bible creates the theological problem.[88] Classical approach holds the Bible as utterly revealed by God from beyond. On this basis, it claims the infallibility and inerrancy of the Bible in the theological advance. In return, such understanding brings forth the acceptance of the literal meaning of the Bible.[89] Therefore, those Christians who fall under the category of classical approach try to sort out the social issues under the guidance of the Bible.[90] Among the scholars, Karl Barth is one who confidently stresses that the Bible has the complete authority over the Church and its policy making.[91]

3.2.1.2 Supernatural Power

Theological method 'from above' tends to locate things in a supernatural way, which we cannot grasp with our five humanly natural senses. For example, 'faith healing' and 'prophecy'[92] are very common practices which powers are supposedly coming through the power of God and the Holy Spirit. In such Christian approach, 'born

---

[87] Karl Barth, 1933, op. cit., 10.

[88] Cf. 'Scripture', in *New Dictionary of Theology*, 640.

[89] 'Doctrine of Scripture', in *The Westminster Dictionary of Christian Theology*, edited by Alan Richardson John Bowden (Philadelphia: The Westminster Press, 1983), 592.

[90] The acceptance of the infallible and inerrancy of the Bible is spelled out in the 'Fundamentalism', 'Eastern Orthodox Theology' and 'Evangelical Theology', in *New Dictionary of Theology*.

[91] John Webster, *Karl Barth* (London: Biddles Ltd, 2000), 56.

[92] 'Prophecy' as bringing the word from God telling what to do and what to happen by somebody. This kind of practice is very much popular in North East India too.

again', cleansing sin, salvation, 'going to heaven or hell', and 'casting demon' alike are the important subjects ever emphasized.[93] Reacting against it, Schleiermacher adamantly rejected the reality of miracles believing in a sense of special acts that abrogate the order of nature. He stated that praying to God to change the course of situations implies that God is somehow dependent on the person praying. In this way, he considered the whole notion of the supernatural power to be dangerous because we cannot know even a single instance of it, and we are nowhere required to recognize it in a humanly natural cognition.[94]

3.2.1.3 Traditional Value

Christian traditional values are important because they bring people close to God by observing them. They measure the value of worship to God. They include all kinds of ritual and practice and belief systems. In the other words, the tradition is "kept alive by the transmission of rite, myths, symbols, stories, doctrine, cult and custom, [and] also by the Holy Scripture and their exposition."[95] It is enormously dynamic in shaping theological norms. Therefore, it is remarkable that the authority of tradition or Church hierarchy controls theology before Enlightenment period. However, Albrecht Ritschl considered such ancient traditions and even the absolute authority of the Bible as 'husk' hiding the pure 'kernel' truth within them. Consequently, many modern scholars moved forward to criticize and reconstruct traditional beliefs centering all theological discourses around the

---

[93] This kind of Christian approach is apparent even in Asia. As a Pastor, Ock Soo Park also always uses as tool to win people to Christian folks exemplified in a sermon book, *The Secrete of Forgiveness and Being Born Again 1,* edited by Wook Yong Kim (Seoul: Good News Publishing House, 1997).

[94] Friedrich Schleiermacher, *The Christian Faith*, Second ed., (Edinburgh: T & T Clark, 1948), 180 & 183.

[95] 'Society and Tradition', in *The Encyclopedia of Christianity,* vol. 5, (Si-Z), edited by Eerdmans Brill (Boston: William B. Eerdmans Publishing Company, 2008), 517.

concept of the kingdom of God, which is continuity rather than the discontinuity between God and humankind.[96]

3.2.2 The Basis of Modern Approach

Modern approach is parallel with classical approach in the sense that there is no meeting point at all. For it is how we assume that modern approach is the offshoot of immanence, whereas, classical is of transcendence. In relative sense, what is emphasized in one approach is not necessarily significant in the other approach. Therefore, their respective influences have impacted on the belief system of the strands of believers.

3.2.2.1 Authority of the Reason

The period of enlightenment, known as the Age of Reason marks the completion of departure from the ancient to the modern eras. The priority of this era is to elevate the power of human reason to seek to understand the truth given through revelation. It emphasizes on the voice of reason within instead of the voice of God from above.[97] As a result, the traditional authority of the Bible is always questioned by modern approach. To Paul Tillich, revelation does not contradict the structure of cognitive reason otherwise; it would be beyond our human understanding to receive it.[98] Besides, Immanuel Kant arose to keep the traditional understanding of the Bible within the limits of the reason. His critical study of pure reason had made the approval of reason and mind in the knowing process. His method of philosophy, 'from reason to revelation', has become remarkable towards replacement of the traditional method 'from revelation to reason' eventually.[99]

---

[96] Refer "Albrecht Ritschl and Classical Liberal Theology: The Immanence of God in Ethical Culture", in *20th Century Theology,* op. cit., 52.

[97] Albrecht Ritschl and Classical Liberal Theology: 'The Enlightenment: The Shattering of the Classical Balance', in *20th Century Theology*, 17.

[98] Paul Tillich, 1954, op. cit., 83-84.

[99] David A. Palin, 'Reason in Relation to Scripture and tradition', in *Scripture, Tradition and Reason: A Study in the Criteria of Christian Doctrine,* edited by Richard Bauckham and Benjamin Drewery (Edinburgh: T & T Clark, 1988), 220-221.

3.2.2.2 'Natural Power'

'Natural power' connotes human power, which is the opposite of supernatural power. The belief of human power in seeking the truth begins from Kant up to the modern scholars. It relies on normal potential or human rationality rooted into anthropocentricism and metaphysics.[100] From this point of view, religion, theology and revelation are never based on mystical understanding. Hegel states that religion is ultimate of thought that seeks to represent the same truth with philosophy. So, he considered philosophical truth as the union of God and humanity.[101] In addition, Schleiermacher even actuates supernatural power as the meeting point between natural science and religion, the meeting point that is humanly rationalized.[102]

3.2.2.3 Conventional Value

Conventional value would mean the life experience in the human history. It cultivates the value of worship to God through what we experience, of joy and sorrow, spelt out by certain contextual theologies like Asian Theology, Latin American Theology, African Theology, Filipino Theology, etc. For instance, black theology reads the word of God in favor of the liberation of the Black community, and feminist theology is witnessing the gender discrimination.[103] Besides, Dalit theology confronts to liberate Dalits from the clutch of Hindu caste system.[104] Therefore, such approach makes sure that God is with human struggle in the world history. This understanding is wrought out mostly by liberal theologians. These contextual theologies under consideration would fall under the ambit of modern approach which emphasizes on belief and practice "from below" and

---

[100] Immanuel Kant, 'Introduction', in *Religion within the Limits of Reason Alone,* (New York: Harper and Row, 1960), xxxi.

[101] G.W.F. Hegel, 'The Immanence of God in Speculative Reason', in *20th Century Theology*, 36.

[102] Friedrich Schleiermacher, 1948, op. cit., 183.

[103] Kuncheria Pathil and Dominic Veliath, 2003, op. cit., 110-112.

[104] Timothy Gorringe, 'Slouching towards Jerusalem: Achieving Human Equality', in *Public Theology for the 21st Century,* edited by William F. Storrar and Andrew R. Morton (New York: T & T Clark, 2004), 317.

believes in realism and pragmatism. This approach is indeed the opposite of the classical approach which depends on the belief 'from above' and mostly considers things in idealism and optimism.

3.2.3 Analysis of the Two Approaches

In the analysis, it will be worth mentioning that the characteristics of classical approach are always understood in opposition to modernity. However, in fact, modern approach develops along with modernity to address any current issue in the twentieth century. Competitively, both approaches are at high level in dealing with the concepts of every visible and invisible thing. Being parallel to each other, they offer us an opportunity to choose either one of the concepts for both religious and spiritual spheres in a distinct way. For a better comparative analysis of the two approaches and their distinguishing features, we shall consider the perspective of justice of compensation and neighborly love.

3.2.3.1 Emotional Attachment

The classical approach on justice of compensation and neighborly love is ambiguous in nature. Of course, it does not deny the relationship between them. However, its attempt tends to detach from the present context of this world. In the classical approach, the attempt is obvious in identifying justice of compensation and neighborly love. The dictum of this approach is - "love is in justice and vice versa". However, there is no clear-cut understanding between them. Thus, Emil Brunner rightly pointed out that Reinhold Niebuhr did not give adequate concept of justice. The understanding of justice and love always overlaps as would find in the statement - "love is both the fulfillment and the negation of justice."[105] Therefore, the classical approach tends to overreact to dramatize the understanding of the Bible, supernatural power and traditional value among others. It tries to promote uncertainty in the decision-making at the moment of any crime. It possibly directs victim to forgive offender at the cost of love without any offender-compensation frame in return. In doing

[105] Gordon Harland, ed., *The Thought of Reinhold Niebuhr* (New York: Oxford University Press, 1960), 23-24.

so, the relation between victim and offender ends up with emotional attachment. This kind of love is unanimously accepted as emotional love. Love is acted through abstract action.[106]

3.2.3.2 Physical Attachment

In the modern approach, the concepts of compensation and neighborly love are not overlapped with one another. They are just like two faces of a coin. The rallying point of this approach is "love is with justice and vice versa". The two concepts are inextricably linked. On this relationship, Augustine opined that love is the inner motivation - the basic impulse, whereas, justice is the directive action in a concrete term. He illustrates with an experiential example: "when I come across a wounded person, I am motivated to love because of the helpless condition, and after which I definitely turn to help because of love."[107] Therefore, one could boldly claim that justice fulfills love. In the other words, one could also claim that without justice, the destination of love cannot be justified. In accordance with criminal justice, it is ideal that something should compensate for the loss at the cost of love. Justice need not be negated but be adjusted to a considerable degree. Love always keeps justice to be flexible and considerable in policies, laws and institutions. With such emphasis, liberal concept of justice of compensation and neighborly love endeavors to concretize the understanding of the Bible, supernatural power and traditional value. It tries to promote physical attachment through certain experience of joy and sorrow in the human history.[108]

3.3 Justice of Compensation in the Light of Christian Love

In the light of Christian love, the act of justice of compensation is not pressurized by any judicial imposition but by the motivation to help the needy. At the moment of crime, victim and offender are considered as both neighbors to each other. Victim, as the neighbor

---

[106] Cf. Roger H. Crook, *Introduction to Christian Ethics,* 105.

[107] Hunter Mabry, ed., *Christian Ethics: An Introductory Reader*, 471.

[108] Walter, G. Muelder, *Moral Law in Christian Social Ethics* (Virginia: John Knox Press, 1966), 170.

of offender deserves to be helped and offender, as the neighbor of victim deserves to be forgiven. From this point of view, compensation is very much significant at the situation of crime.

3.3.1 Compensation in the Face of Forgiveness

The crime, from the perspective of Christian love is considered as the creation of broken relationship between individuals, within an individual and society, or between individuals and God. This brokenness is restored by reconciling love of God that is shown through incarnation and crucifixion. God forgives our sin forgetting the punishment deserved for committing sin. This idea of forgiveness is what is to be followed. In the way God treats us we also must treat someone who deserves punishment for evil act. However, it is to be understood that reconciliation is understood as both a gift and judicial act worked through the righteousness of God. Therefore, forgiveness under judicial act has to follow proper conviction for an offence.[109] Offender has to acknowledge the committed action and the responsibility towards the victim. This is exactly meant by justice of compensation to be offered by offender. By compensation only, offender can feel free of being guilty, even if s/he is forgiven considering her or him as the enemy of victim. Yet, anyhow, forgiveness cannot be enforced at the cost of compensation. It is indebted to the one who becomes an enemy of someone by committing an offence. Likewise, compensation is indebted to the one who becomes a neighbor of someone by facing an offence. Under this circumstance, Christian love works out right for both victim and offender. Without it, victim may remain in the position of loss, and offender, in the position of punishment. Besides, forgiveness and compensation may not be at the point of neighborhood.

3.3.2 Compensation as Responsibility

Generally, there is a human tendency and feeling to avenge the one who hurts as far as retribution is effective because no one wants to get hurt without any cause. 'Eye for eye'[110] is a common code that carries

---

[109] Christ Wood, 1991, op. cit., 82-83.

[110] 'Eye for eye' connotes 'Tit for tat'.

the whole idea of retaliation. We can even say that the whole Bible is filled with retributive idea as the means to resolve the problem of crime. In the Old Testament, Mosaic Law spells out the purpose of '*lex talionis*' and in the New Testament, Apostle Paul resounds this by being ready to accept the charge against him even up to the extent of death if he deserves death for the deeds done. Nevertheless, in the Bible, retaliation is always discouraged by such a word, 'vengeance is mine...'.[111] On the other hand, there are verses that indicate 'not to repay evil for evil' in the New Testament. Accordingly, we are advised to admit to the Biblical prohibition of retaliation in Christian praxis. Then, it is asked what for the compensation is. It is the recognition of what the offender has done to the victim and of self-transformation in the society on the one hand. On the other, it is how offender has to respond to victim as responsibility in the similar way that victim offers forgiveness as responsibility.[112]

3.3.3 Compensation as Compromise

Compromise is an act of reconciliation, which is an ongoing process to be completed through human reasoning effort including forgiveness and reconciliation.[113] Biblically, reconciliation overcomes hostilities, suspicions, barriers and dividing wall of partition between Jew and Gentile, male and female and slave and free. God accepts us so as to enable us to accept and serve one another irrespective of pairs of opposites – black and white, straight and gay, rich and poor, criminals and respectable citizens. In such case, compromise is considered to be the best way to solve the problem between victim and offender. It is as the capacity measured to be proportionate between two parties by scaling down certain amount. Applying this, both victim and offender have to relegate their positions and minimize what they wish

---

[111] Lex talionis in Exod. 21:23-25 and Act. 25:11 and Vengeance in Deut. 32:35, Rom. 12:19 and Heb. 10:30 (NRSV).

[112] Richard Quinney, *Class, State and Crime,* second edition (London: Longman Inc., 1980), 4.

[113] For this perspective, refer Robert Gibbs, 'Philosophy and Law: Questioning justice', in *The Ethical,* edited by Edith Wyschogrod and Gerald P. McKenny (Berlin: Blackwell Publishing Ltd, 2003), 106.

through negotiation and agreement.[114] After which victim is advised to forgive and forget, and in turn, offender is also advised to feel free of blame by compensating. For victim, compensation is the image of love and for offender it is compromise. As a result, they are satisfied with one another despite all immediate painful experience. By such reconciling process, there is complete manifestation of oneness and dependency upon one another in any case.[115]

3.3.4 Compensation, the Power of Mental Healing

Sickness does not encompass the absence of health only but mental absence which contributes to the well-being of a person. According to the World Health Organization (WHO), health is a state of complete physical, mental and social well-being and not merely the absence of disease. To this, spiritual well-being is also added from the point of religion. Biblically, health is connoted with a Hebrew word, 'shalom' translated as 'peace' derived from 'soundness' or 'well-being' in English.[116] From this perspective, we understand that both victim and offender feel mentally disturbed as soon as the crime takes place. Definitely, victim has the feeling of rejection due to the injury that deforms her /his well-being. Offender also has the feeling of fear and guilt due to the evil act that deforms the same. The impending consequences whether from the victim or God are awaited. Thus, compensation is necessary as the power of healing process for both victim and offender. Without which they will be in the stage of confusion. Compensation helps victim to be released from feeling rejection and helps the physical healing process.[117] It also helps offender to be released from guilt, shame and fear of consequence. Beside forgiveness, it motivates offender to forget the offending act and to have a positive contact with victim without any hesitation.

---

[114] http://www.johnhoward.ab.ca/pub/pdf/c27.pdf (12 December 2010).

[115] Christ Wood, 1991, op. cit., 89-90.

[116] See 'Healing', in *New Dictionary of Theology*, 287-288.

[117] http:cvaconline.org/resources/thefinalthesis.pdf (17 December 2010).

Therefore, compensation has become the power of healing that reinstitutes the well-being of both victim and offender.[118]

3.3.5 Compensation, the Expression of True Love

Forgiveness from one side alone does not solve the problem of crime without compensation. According to neighborly love, both victim and offender are neighbors to each other through forgiveness and compensation. By such actions, the feeling of loss and wicked deed can be wiped away at least to an extent, and the broken relationship is restored without any further confusion. In this stance, love would be superficial and fake without the practice of forgiveness and compensation. For agape, as the highest good can only exist along with eternal restoration and relationship between God and the people and between people and others that God has made.[119] Agape is a matter of blood and flesh experiences. Restoring the whole world to the right relationship with God, Jesus shed his blood and shattered his flesh on the cross. This background empowers how we restore our broken relationship through different faces of crime. In such case, an offender is not free by forgiveness. At least s/he has to turn to restore the usual relationship with victim through help in the form of compensation due to love. Such love is thought of true love grown through bad situation. In fact, it is hard for the offender to give compensation to victim in the situation of crime. However, in doing so, it becomes the expression of true love, which we ever consider as the highest good in Christian life.[120]

3.4 Necessity of Justice of Compensation in the Crime

According to biblical explanation, God is love,[121] and love has become the most important object in Christian life. Apostle Paul strengthens

---

[118] Karin Granberg-Michaelson, *Healing Community* (Geneva: WCC Publications, 1991), 73-74.

[119] Cf. Tina Chanter, 'Kristeva's Ethics of Crisis: Art and Abjection, Love and Melancholia', in *The Ethical*, 129.

[120] James Walter Gustafson with Joseph B. Onyango-Okello, *The Quest for Truth: An Introduction to Philosophy*, 168-169.

[121] I John 4:8 (NRSV).

it by saying that faith, hope and love abide, and the greatest of these is love. There is no problem with love because it alone goes into eternity.[122] Nevertheless, the problem lies with the question whether it is with or without action. Without action, love becomes superficial, and it becomes nothing but ridiculous especially in the situation of crime. Just loving everybody cannot be the meaning of love. There should be a certain reason like, need, sickness, helplessness, etc., which attracts people to love in a concrete term. This is categorically stated by the author in the letter of James written to progress towards Christian maturity. In the letter, he deliberately mentioned the law of liberty that Christians had to follow focusing on love for the neighbor. Besides, he urged that Christians have to be doers, not hearers to the word of God which is phrased 'faith that works.'[123] It seems that the number of the poor was high in the Christian community during the ministry of James.[124] Consequently, he advised the readers to meet the needs of the poor; otherwise their faith would become useless and dead. This suggests that faith has to be accompanied by action without which faith is dead as the body without spirit.[125] Of course, James did not explain about love in every detail. However, his approach of dealing with the community aimed at the true meaning of love, especially neighborly love.

With this principle, justice of compensation and neighborly love are expected to rule over crime. Unless the offender exercises this principle of love at the situation of crime what would love mean for her or him? Moreover, unless the offender is attracted to the wound as the cause to love victim what would be the meaning of love for her or him? It follows that if the offender does not follow justice of compensation, love is worthless to her or him. Besides, as a social conscious being, the human status in her or him would also be tantamount to death. Such person then deserves to be taught as a beginner or a neophyte. Besides, if any society declines such

---

[122] D.A. Carson, *Showing the Spirit: A Theological Exposition of I Corinthians 12-14* (Michigan: Baker Books, 1987), 72.

[123] Douglas J. Moo, *The Letter of James* (Leicester: Apollos, 2000), 37.

[124] Michael J. Townsend, *The Epistle of James* (London: Epworth Press, 1989), 44.

[125] Douglas J. Moo, 2000, op. cit, 119.

principle of justice and love, it deserves to take advice for it. Finally, whichever school of thought and theology that does not touch this ground reality need to reconstruct and/or review as far as possible.

3.5 Conclusion

The way to understanding things irrespective of visible and invisible relations depends on theoretical or conceptual frame. Every structured meaning reveals the etymological essence. The particular Christian understanding of thing goes back to Christian schools of thought coming down from ages namely, Transcendent and Immanent bases by which Christians reproduced two theological approaches 'from above' and 'from below' competitively. Christians follow their characteristics to interpret the Bible consistently. The question of choice to employ these two schools of thought and theology can be paradoxical. Besides, the method to employ these thoughts is being doubted as their aspirations do not reach the human experience. This is the challenge that has ever come in the form of 'classical' and 'modern approaches', with their unique supporters without compromise in this Christian era. For instance, they set apart the understandings of justice of compensation and neighborly love from each other. The group under classical approach displays its understandings in an emotional aspect. And the group under modern approach displays the understandings in a physical aspect. From one side, love is accepted as unconditional or limitless, and from the other side it is considered as conditional or limited. Under this circumstance, it is simply accepted that classical approach embraces love in abstract feature, whereas modern approach considers love as a concrete feature, particularly, to address any social issue. In this approach, justice of compensation is viewed as nothing more than concrete action that creates the reality of love. Its principle carries forgiveness, personal responsibility, compromise, healing and the meaning of neighborly love in the situation of crime. More than rule, it is but a phase of meaning and value of life by helping one another in time of need.[126] In general, such is the heart of the Gospel that the

[126] Steve Herman with Gregg Stebben, *Everything You Need to Know About Philosophy* (Singapore: Pocket Books, 1999), 23.

author of letter to James ever urged the readers to live. This principle can be applied in addressing rape cases. The relevance of this principle to rape cases shall be discussed in the following Chapter.

Chapter 4

The Context of Rape

4.1 Introduction

Rape is taking place in most of the places of this world. It is believed that it will not be possible for us to stop it except decreasing the number of its cases. In fact, despite different strategies, the number of cases does not decrease, but it seems to increase. In such situation, there is a question to ask on the law and order of the state. One could say that it is due to the weakness of law and order, by and large. Law and order needs both levels of strategy – the strategy to prevent rape and the strategy to handle the cases. Until and unless they are looked into carefully and without partisan the incidence of rape will continue to be there frequently, and justice may be denied most of the time. At this point, it will be relevant and profitable to focus on the strategy to handle the case in order to achieve justice as far as retributive justice is concerned.[127] Here, justice is meant to

[127] Retributive justice is noted under the 'casuistic law' in order to deal with crime. In case there is no crime, such law is of no use. It is mainly made for the achievement of equal justice between victim and offender in any crime.

equalize both rape victims and rapists by obligating compensation as the means to solution of the case. While dealing with the strategy, an attempt shall be made to justify how true love is seen at the face of compensation in any crime, particularly the crime of rape.

There are different kinds and dimensions of rape. There are variations even within the same kind of rape. As a result, it may cause ambiguity in discussion of rape without classifying all the differences. Rape does not take place between different sexes alone but in the same sex as well. The meaning of rape even includes mouth play beside genital sex *inter alia*. It happens not only in open relatives but close relatives and within family members too. There is no specific age in rape. Rapists may be counted from teenage to old age and rape victims, from childhood to old age. In this Chapter only one kind of rape- *genital sex* between open relatives shall be considered. For illustrative purpose, the Indian situation of rape cases shall be drawn.[128] The Indian Penal Code (IPC) shall also be highlighted as a legal entity in rape cases. Finally, the principle of justice of compensation and neighborly love shall be applied towards delivery of justice in rape crime. This application shall mainly focus on decision-making to resolve problem between rape victims and rapists.

4.2 Rape

Rape is one of the most heinous and common crimes happening generation after generations in every corner of the world despite different strategies resorted to stop them. It is believed that it will be impossible to prevent it totally but to work towards reducing the number of cases. Thus, it reflects how important it is to handle rape case in a judicious manner.

Even though it is generally agreed that rape is a violent crime,[129] the definitions of rape differ from state to state. However, it generally

---

[128] Since the content of rape differs from one state to another, the detail cannot be worked out. But the situation of rape in India is taken just as an example to show the slight picture of rape in this book.

[129] J. Kerby Anderson, *Moral Dilemmas: Biblical Perspectives on Contemporary Ethical Issues* (Nashville: Word Publishing, 1998), 86.

refers to penetration of the penis into the vagina, mouth or anus against the will of the victim by force or threat.[130] According to the Indian Penal Code, Section 375, the definition of rape falls under the following circumstances.

First - Against her will.
Second - Without her consent.
Third - With her consent [under the circumstance of any threat and any drug or stupefying element].
Fourth - With or without her consent, when she is under sixteen years of age.[131]

According to a source, it is said that every fifty four minutes one female is raped in India.[132] A latest source noted from National Crime Records Bureau Statistics says that more than fifty three rape cases are recorded everyday in India. It also shows the weakness and problem with the police in handling the rape cases. While victims are known to rapists in ninety percent of rape cases, the victims' families fail to fight for justice. Therefore, it is observed that there is an urgent need for police reforms with proper mechanism for efficient implementation. It also calls for establishing fast track courts and trauma-rehabilitation centers countrywide, and sex education in colleges and schools should be introduced to bring speedy solution.[133]

4.3 Manifestation of Rape

The study about the manifestation of rape may be wide in ranging. For rape has been taking place everywhere since immemorial time in whatsoever manner. As a result, there seems to be no safety place for

---

[130] Marie M. Fortune, *Sexual Violence: The Unmentionable Sin* (Ohio: The Pilgrim Press, 1983), 7 & 8.

[131] See Agnes Flavia, ed., *Journey to Justice: Procedures to be Followed in a Rape Case* (Mumbai: N.P., 1990), 12.

[132] Refer 'One rape every 54 minutes', in *Women and Rape* (Pune: Streevani Documentation Centre – 1991 – 1993), 16.

[133] "Fight Rapes: Speedy justice key to combating sexual crimes', in *The Times of India* (Bangalore), 11 February 2011, 16.

female. From childhood to adulthood, they are all alarmed of fear of rape everywhere. It is because of the fact that rape associates with brutal acts and death. There are ample incidences of this pathetic situation that can be cited. As of these cases, we can cite the recently reported incidence where the rapist chopped off a Dalit girl's nose, ear and parts of her hand due to resisting rape in Utter Pradesh. In yet another case, a girl was pushed out of a running train and raped in Kerala.[134] Besides, it is so frequent to publicize of female murder irrespective of age after rape.These cases also substantiate that there is no specific place and time for rape. For better understanding, we shall consider some of the contexts.

4.3.1 Within Family

Female members are not safe even in their own family because different types of rape can possibly take place within the family such as in between father-daughter, mother-son, brother-sister rape and so on. In this way, the male members in a family can become rapists and female members as rape victims. Evidently, there is full of father-daughter rape case noted in the book, 'When Fathers Rape', starting from Jeet Singh Chauhan who was arrested for raping his minor daughters.[135] Besides, there are more reports like about rape taking place between father-in-law and a girl[136] and father and stepdaughter (15 years old).[137] This is the scenario of rape taking place within family.

---

[134] This source is found in the same paragraph of 'Fight Rapes: Speedy justice key to combating sexual crimes', in *The Times of India* (Bangalore), 11 February 2011, 16.

[135] 'The World of Parental Rapes: Where Humans do not exist', in *When the Fathers Rape: A Socio-psycho-legal-global Study,* edited by Manish Sharma (New Delhi: A.P.H. Publishing Corporation, 1996), 3.

[136] M.U. Qureshi, *Women and Crime* (New Delhi: Chaman Enterprises, 2006), 326.

[137] *A Lesser Child: Girl Child in India*, Readings on Women Studies Series: 7 (Bombay: Research Centre for Women's Studies at Shreemati Nathibai Damodar Thackersey Women's University, n.d), 50.

4.3.2 Outside Family

It has been generally observed that it is more awesome for women to be outside than to be inside the boundary of family. Outside the family, rapists can be anyone from different communities, and rape can happen whenever and wherever they are. Therefore, excluding the place, rapists can be understood from two dimensions, such as, 'ordinary men' and 'authority figures'.

4.3.2.1 Ordinary Man

The term 'ordinary man' includes all strangers, friends and colleagues. Being strangers and friends, the rapists usually follow women and take opportunity of rape at bus or train stations, streets, fields and even in their own house.[138] Here, when a girl is raped by her friend, the victim is reluctant to expose it thinking that even if she tells it will not be believed since she has a relationship with that person.[139] Gang rape usually happens outside family under the scheme of ordinary men.

4.3.2.2 Authority Figure

Here, the authority may an employer, doctor, minister, teacher, etc., who takes care of others including female. In the trap of such person, rape usually happens at job's place, school and college, hospital, and any other institution. Such rape is known as custodial rape that incurs more serious punishment than the normal rape.[140] Rape by the help of drug may take place in both within and outside family.

4.4 Causes of Rape

Rape has a multitude of factors by nature. As a result, one theory cannot explain all rape cases. Regarding the causes of rape, there are several reasons behind the rapists. Every rapist has different motives

---

[138] M.U. Qureshi, 2006, op. cit., 325.

[139] Marie M. Fortune, 1983, op. cit., 142.

[140] Multiple Action Research Group, *Rape Kidnapping and Abduction: Our Laws 9* (New Delhi: Print Art, 1992), 14.

in committing rape at different time. However, it is obvious that several cultural factors seem to contribute to rape.

4.4.1 Myth

There is a common myth as such -

- A man must have sex to prove his masculinity;
- When women say no to sex, they really mean yes, so men should ignore women's refusals;
- If a woman engages in kissing or petting, she is obligated to engage in sexual intercourse.[141]

4.4.2 Lust

Humans have the gift of lust, which depends on the role of hormones, Testosterone in male and Estrogen in female.[142] And there are some reasons that arouse lust, like perfumes, drugs/alcohols, and provocative dresses. It is said that the chemical like perfumes and drugs/alcohol can induce hormones effectively. Therefore, when some men are in contact with such atmosphere, their libido flares out eventually. Besides, women's provocative behavior erodes men's resistance and that leads to rape.[143] So, rape has become a means to fulfill someone's sexual desire.

4.4.3 Domination

The cause of rape is also related to structure and system of society. Many societies are male-dominated societies. Regarding sexuality, the directive control of female reproductive power has been central to the foundation of male authority. Sexual act remains exclusively for male right and vocation. Naturally, it has to do with male pleasure

---

[141] http://family.jrank.org/pages/1350/Rape-Causes-Rape.html (12 February 2011).

[142] Pepper Schwartz and Virginia Rutter, *The Gender of Sexuality* (New Delhi: Pine Forge Press, 1998), 6.

[143] http://www.backlash.com/book/rape6.html (13 February 2011).

and conquest.[144] Basing on such motive, women are considered as cheap as object.

4.4.4 Ethnic Cleansing

It is not strange that rape is used as weapon of war. In some places, many women happen to be raped at the motive of 'ethnic cleansing'. For instance, Serbian troops used to raid houses and raped numbers of nuns and Muslim women in Bosnia. It is said that the estimates of pregnant rape victims range from 27,000 to 50,000.[145]

4.4.5 Economic Pressure

It is not a surprise to say that men usually pay price whether in marriage or in prostitution depending on the price average in the market. When the price soars up, it is recorded that the rate of rape increases. It could be the reason when some men from poor family cannot afford the current amount. Surveys of the socioeconomic status of rapists in the United State, cross-cultural studies from Denmark and Australia confirm that majority unskilled, unemployed, and poorly educated males are more often rapists.[146]

4.5 Sexuality

Sexuality of human being can be understood from different perspectives. For the purpose of this discussion, we shall limit to the theological perspective. This perspective begins with the assumption that sexuality is characteristic of all human beings. It would also mean that the power of one's sex drive is unrelated to others. Sexuality is considered good and is not necessarily evil. So, it should be saved from jealousies, frustrations and insecurities that break personal relationship. Its root meaning derives from the common biblical term for the legitimate sexual relationship 'to know', which propagates two basic functions – reproduction and maintenance of union of two

---

[144] V. Geetha, *Patriarchy: Theorizing Feminism* (Calcutta: Bhatkal and Sen, 2007), 166-167.

[145] Refer 'If a Sister Becomes Pregnant, We'll Help Her to Childbirth' – The horror story of nuns in Bosnia', in *Women and Rape,* 7.

[146] http://www.backlash.com/book/rape6.html, (16 February 2011).

individuals. In this case, man and woman do not come together to fulfill their sexual desires alone but to be united as one. Nevertheless, sexual drive has to be regulated naturally as satisfying the hunger for food without which sexual repression would be as dangerous as sexual license. It holds that sexuality being natural God's gift, any kind of sexual force is a violation of a person and God's will.[147]

Deviating from 'traditional sexual ethics', 'sexual revolution' had turned ethical point of human nature into individualistic and naturalistic model. It extends sexual gratification and pleasure as natural and cultural. For instance, contraceptive and abortive technology can limit offspring from the consequence of sexual activity. Thus, it is argued that individuals have a natural right to seek sexual fulfillment.[148] Such is the basis on which sexuality minorities stands against Judeo-Christian morality, Hindu Manusmrithi and Islamic Shariat law and others that limit the concept of human sexuality. By way of its negative attitude, such minorities were being discriminated severely even in India.[149] However, as a positive response to their movements Government had sanctioned legal measure against discrimination in IPC which reads:

> *Same sex marriages should be recognized as legal and valid; all legal benefits, including property rights that accrue to heterosexual married people should be made available to same-sex unions.*[150]

Sex ethics is also largely related to the ethos of society and culture. This is for the fact that civilization requires restriction of sexual opportunity as even Sigmund Freud also agreed even if he

---

[147] Roger H. Crook, 2002, op. cit., 119-121.

[148] Victor Preller, O.G.S., 'Sexual Ethics and the Single Life', in *Men and Women: Sexual Ethics in Turbulent Times,* edited by Philip Turner (Massachusetts: Cowley Publications, 1989), 118.

[149] 'Sexuality minorities' is an inclusive term of gays, lesbians, bisexuals, transgenders, hijras and others, in Human Rights Violations against Sexuality Minorities in India, *Fact-finding Report about Bangalore* (A PUCL-K), 9-10.

[150] 'Sexuality minorities' is an inclusive term of gays, lesbians, bisexuals, transgenders, hijras and others, Human Rights Violations against sexuality Minorities in India, *Fact-finding Report about Bangalore,* 56-57.

regarded sexual repression being harmful.[151] Under this circumstance, IPC rightly spells out 'rape against her will' as being unnatural beyond human toleration.

4.6 Levels of Rape Trauma

M.U. Qureshi (2006) points out three levels of rape trauma such as psychological, physical and social aspects. Besides, spiritual aspect is also one of the levels that cannot be omitted. Therefore, it will be pertinent to discuss the four levels of trauma faced by rape victims.

4.6.1 Psychological Aspect

Psychological disturbance caused by rape is seen in three ways as before, during and after rape. Usually, every female is always alarmed of rape even before rape. They are not free of the fear of rape. During rape, the victim takes the risk of personal, social and physical stigmas by surrendering and resisting rape.[152] After rape, criminal justice system, social stigma and physical injury lead her to distrusting in men and society and confronting the difficulties of sexual adjustment. As psychological effect, she suffers from fear, insomnia, anxiety and hallucination, among others that possibly lead her up to the level of taking refuge in suicide.

4.6.2 Physical Aspect

Rape victim suffers a wide range of physical injuries depending on the location and the extent of resistance. Physical attacks of the rapist generally hurt throat, neck, cheeks, thighs, legs, arms and genitals of the victim. After rape, physical complaint of pain begins in different parts of the body such as skeletal muscle tension, gastro-intestinal irritability and genitor-urinary disturbances.

---

[151] V.A. Demant, *Christian Sex Ethics: An Introduction* (Evanston: Harper and Row Publishers, 1963), 94-96.

[152] This is a dilemma between if she surrenders sexually, her life is going to be spoilt, and if she resists rape, she is going to face an attack of rapist.

4.6.3 Social Aspect

Whether married or unmarried, child or adult, victim is socially mistreated. If a victim is married, there is a chance of breaking the marriage bond. Even if marital life continues the chances of restoring to normal life is very dim or it is hardly possible due to various stigma. If she is unmarried, she worries about marriage in the near future. Rape is unbearable for family members too. The prestige of family is also lowered in the society. In such a male-dominated society, rapists remain as they are, but victims are subjected to all sorts of weaknesses – physical, social and psychological.[153]

4.6.4 Spiritual Aspect

Misfortune or accident always encounters spiritual predicament. In such case, rape victim always asks, 'Why does God let it happen to us?' She often feels if God is punishing her for something done in the past. As a result, there is a high possibility of causing inferior complex and rejection by thinking if it is the will of God.[154] This is the most burdensome moment for victim. As such, she can even remain in a miserable life by quarrelling with God and asking lots of unending questions about life.

4.7 Law and Order in Indian Penal Code

Rape is not just an offence against an individual but also a crime against the state according to criminal justice system of India.[155] Therefore, there are strict laws against rape by imposing various forms of punishment. Depending on the severity of the case IPC sections 376, 376A, 376B, 376C, 376D, 354, 377 and 509 are imposed where the maximum punishment is imprisonment of one to five years which are either bailable or non-bailable.[156] On the other hand, it is also found that the punishment of rape is imprisonment for at least seven years or up to ten years depending on the conditions

---

[153] M.U. Qureshi, 2006, op. cit., 328-332.

[154] Marie M. Fortune, 1983, op. cit., 154.

[155] Flavia, ed., 1990, op. cit., 17.

[156] Flavia, ed., 1990, op. cit., 22-23.

– becoming pregnant, victim of below twelve years, gang rape and custodial rape.[157] Accordingly, imprisonment is mostly practiced as a form of punishment for rape in India. Very recently, it is reported that the rapists of 26 years old from Jharkhand are arrested to custody[158] and another source reported that one of them may have been gunned down as punishment in Bangalore.[159] However, it is not clear as to what kind of punishment it has been awarded.

Regarding monetary aspect, a source reported that (1) an accused was fined Rs. 2,500/- out of which Rs. 1,500/- to be paid to the victim in 1986 in Rajasthan. (2) For Gang rape, four accused were charged with Rs. 5000/- each and the leader would pay Rs. 10,000/- along with compensation as per the court judgment in 1988 in Kerala. (3) In addition, the accused had to bear fine of Rs. 5000/- to be paid to victim as compensation for the prospect of marriage and wiping out the anguish in 1988 in Orissa. They were all passed through High court according to Criminal Procedure Code (CrPC) as per section 357 in order to resolve the case.[160] Apart from the IPC it is practiced in community level to settle the case. For instance, a community panchayat at Dadheru in Muzaffarnagar directed a rapist to marry fourteen years old victim. They got married on November 23, 2010 with the help of police.[161] Moreover, it is also practiced to give fine to the victim along with domestic animal as per the plea suiting the custom in some of the tribal areas. This is done through the court only.[162]

[157] Multiple Action Research Group, 1992, op. cit., 13.

[158] 'Police yet to close in on gang that raped woman: Minister, Cops' Statements On Arrests Vary', in *The Times of India* (Bangalore), 18 December 2010, 3.

[159] 'Gang recorded rapes on phones', in *The Times of India* (Bangalore), 21 December 2010, 3.

[160] Flavia, ed., *Journey to Justice,* 61.

[161] 'Rape accused asked to marry victim', in *The Times of India* (Bangalore), 25 November 7.

[162] Flavia, ed., 1990, op. cit., 42.

4.8 Limitations of Law and Order in India

By assessing the reports cited above, one can possibly observe the weakness of law and order mechanism in dealing with rape cases in India. In view of the matter discussed above, the following assumptions could possibly be drawn from the above statement.

- There is no common and strict norm of judgment.
- The security deployment is not sufficient.
- There is a mishandling or manipulation of the case.
- Crime always reflects punishment.
- Above all, the decision-making is based on justice alone, which is inseparable with love.

Despite the prospect of the IPC for efficiency of law and order situation, there appears to be no common norm of judgment to be followed whenever rape takes place. For instance it is uncertain to rule out even what to do with the offenders [Ram Singh, Mukesh, Akshay Thakur, Vinay Sharma, and Pawan Gupta] who are responsible for Nirbhaya's gang rape that leads her to death very recently.[163] In addition, most of the time rape happens where and when police forces do not hang around. It is informed that even if the victim is known to accused in ninety percent of rape cases, there is no speedy recovery. There is always a wave of careless investigation and manipulation of cases with police in court. Sometime even if the complaint is registered, it takes even up to a year for the police to take the matter to the courts.[164] If such is the case, then, where is the justice towards the victim? Moreover, where is the dimension of love in such case? In order to address these crucial questions it will be appropriate to consider the principles of justice of compensation and neighborly love in decision-making of such case.

---

[163] 'Ordinance moots death if rape victim dies or goes into coma: Voyeurism, Stalking Made Specific Crimes' in *The Times of India*, (New Delhi), 2nd February 2013, 1.

[164] Refer 'Rape Cases Justice on Trial', in *Women and Rape*, 13.

4.9 Application of Justice of Compensation and Neighborly Love

It is believed that the principles of justice of compensation and neighborly love are appropriate enough in dealing with the decision-making of rape case. The reasons to apply such principles are to overthrow any attempt of decision-making based on retributive justice, to elevate obligatory compensation on rapist as a common norm representing justice and love and to decide the case depending on the conditions of rape victim and rapist.

4.9.1 Kinds of Compensation

Here, I propose five kinds of compensation to be carried out by rapists in a strict manner. They are monetary compensation, property shift, bond labor, marriage arrangement and imprisonment.

4.9.1.1 Monetary Compensation

Monetary compensation is being practiced as a best possible means to solve the case of rape in every state from the beginning dates like Ancient Near East (ANE).[165] It is implemented everywhere under different rates given by the court or any other institution. Now, it is high time to deliberate on how far the awarded rates of rape charge in different states meet the demands of justice. For instance, a case of gang rape that verifies the amount of Rs. 5000/- each from the rapist and Rs. 10,000/- from the first rapist decided through High court under section 357 CrPC as noted above.[166] Can we say that it is feasible amount of rape charge to be handed over to a rape victim? Do the amounts serve justice of equality for both victim and rapist? Here, it is suggested that the possible rate should be a standard size depending on the conditions of both sides under justice and equality. In any case, monetary compensation should not be exempted. It is obligated to rapist.

---

[165] In the Laws oflsnunna and Hittite Codes, monetary compensation was practiced as a form of an ancient corporal punishment. Cf. U. Cassuto, *A Commentary on the Book of Exodus*, 276.

[166] As mentioned above.

4.9.1.2 Property Shift

Property shift is important because it helps the accused to meet the fixed amount of the awarded compensation to be given to rape victim. It depends on the preference whether the rapist wants to do it or have to do it because of economic condition. In case, the accused is not in the position to meet the amount due to financial condition, and wants to give any property equivalent to the fixed amount in place of money it can be done without any hesitation.[167]

4.9.1.3 Bond Labor

The term 'bond labor' may possess negative connotation on the one hand,[168] but it also possesses positive meaning on the other. Positively, it is practiced in order to enhance 'fairness' in the society. From the perspective of justice of compensation, bond labor is meant to work for certain periods of time to catch up the fixed amount of compensation in the condition when rapist cannot pay at the time. The types of bond labor may be manual work working directly at the fields belonging to rape victim or other vocations apart from the victim's fields. This has to be taken care of by the higher authority. In case, the amount is not covered up within the given period due to sickness, death or any other misfortunes, the higher authority is responsible to handle the circumstance whether to extend the duration, to accept the existing amount, to give the responsibility to the near relatives, or to excuse the accused.[169]

---

[167] The formula of retributive justice, 'Eye for eye' or 'Slave for slave' was not strictly observed in the Ancient Near East. It was always replaced by monetary fine in a moderate way. In such case, property shift is quite possible to replace monetary compensation if rapists will or if rapist has a financial constraint. Such moderate or flexible approach is one of the principles of justice of compensation.

[168] A practice during Middles Ages (roughly 9th-14th centuries) to serve lords in feudal society as discussed in Gabriele Dietrich and Bas Wielenga, *Toward Understanding Indian Society* (Kottayam: Wigi Printers, 2003), 93.

[169] Rapists are kept to work until reaching the value of the rape compensation's amount. This is based on a characteristic of bond labor that determines the value of commodity as discussed in Karl Marx, *Wages, Price and Profit: Workers of all Countries, Unite* (Peking: Foreign Languages Press, 1970), 32.

4.9.1.4 Marriage Arrangement

It may or may not be a taboo that virginity is one of the sacred and important elements preserving for marriage in one's life. As a result, loss of virginity gives a negative impact to people especially to rape victim. In this case, if there is an agreement between rape victim and rapist to arrange marriage, it is considered as one of the best forms of compensation in rape case. However, care should be taken; otherwise there may be more violence after marriage.[170] In the case of gang rape, if there is an agreement between rape victim and rapist from among the gang for the proposed method of marriage, it can be done very boldly. In such case, partial amount of the fixed rate of compensation from the rest of gang is to be charged.

4.9.1.5 Imprisonment

Imprisonment is an important option along with monetary compensation. It is included under compensation in order to resist the repeat action of crime. The objectives of imprisonment emphasize on reform, rehabilitation and treatment of criminals. It is also considered as a means to reduce crime rates in the society.[171] It is not done as a mere punishment for the evil act as far as love and justice are expected to co-exist in the crime. "It is a restorative punishment, a punishment that promises healing."[172] Since rape is a brutal crime by nature, the offender deserves to undergo imprisonment for seven to ten years conditional to certain categories - ordinary rape, gang rape, custodian rape and minor rape.[173] In case a rapist repeats the same crime after release, such rapist needs to face life imprisonment. Basing on Bhutan law, if the case is gang rape and murder, the leader

---

[170] http//desicritics.rog/2010/03/27/065314.php (6 January 2011).

[171] Edwin H. Sutherland and Donald R. Cressey, eds., *Principles of Criminology*, sixth edition (New York: J.B. Lippincott Company, 1960), 460-461.

[172] Christopher D. Marshall, 2001, op. cit., 135.

[173] 'The People View: Exclusive Interview with D.C.P and Ex-Chief of Crime (Women) Cell, Ms Yamin Hazarika', in *When the Fathers Rape: A Socio-psycho-legal-global Study*, edited by Manish Sharma, 62.

has to face lifelong imprisonment.[174] The authority has to decide the duration of imprisonment for the rest of the rapists.

4.10 Rate of Rape Compensation

The assessment of the accurate rate of rape compensation is rather difficult as it is not commercial in nature. However, it is one of the purposes of this book to draw out a feasible amount in order to meet characteristics of equality in the face of such crisis. It is suggested that the amount of the compensation can never be the same but it has to be rated according to the class to which they belong.[175] In such case, if the rapist is from high class the amount of the compensation is proposed to be Rs. 500000/- and above, from middle class to be Rs. 300000/- and above, from lower class to be Rs. 10000/- to 50000/-, and from beggars and others to be Rs. 500/- to 10000/.[176] Exceptionally, if

[174] 'Royal Regimes: Amendments for the Offence of Rape under the Marriage Act', in *When the Fathers Rape: A Socio-psycho-legal-global Study*, edited by Manish Sharma, 269.

[175] I simply classify the classes as high, middle, lower and others for analytical convenience. There are, no doubt, different schemes of classification of class. For instance, K.L. Sharma classifies class as consisting agrarian, industrial, professional classes and the business and mercantile classes (see K.L. Sharma, *Social Stratification in India* (New Delhi: Sage Publications, 1997, p. 190).

[176] Normally, there are two kinds of monetary compensations, namely judicial compensation from the government of state and from rapist. The former case is additional /exceptional, while the second one is considered as true compensation. In the case of judicial compensations, there are no fixed amount practiced in India, and it is not comparable to other states too. In India, in 2008, the Court of Punjab approved Rs.1 lac as maximum compensation for the loss of life, Rs.40,000 in case of loss of any limb, Rs.30,000 as compensation for rape and Rs.20,000 for loss of injury causing severe mental agony to women and child victims in case like human trafficking (See http://www.punjabnewsline/com/content/punjab-pat-rs30000-compensation-rapevictims/27467, 6 January 2011). Whereas in other states, the amount of compensation is $31,500 (around Rs. 14,175, 00/-) for rape and $12,750 (around Rs. 5,73,750/-) for injuries suffered during their rape and sexual assault (Refer http://news.ninemsn.com.au/national/1075801/taxpayers-pay-compensation-for-broke-rapist_(6 January 2011). On this basis, the proper amount in the book is perhaps justifiable. The first and second categories of compensation amount are not even big enough for those who belong to high and second classes. However, it will be difficult for such people belonging to other classes to bear the mentioned amounts. As a result, it will be wise to consider their conditions how

the rapist is a big leader who has a big income is proposed to be 10,00000/-,[177] and if a rapist is a stray lunatic, rape victim deserves to get Rs. 500000/- from the state.[178] There may be some rapists who have financial constraint but a big amount of property. This has to be checked and balanced in the decision-making. For the case of gang rape and murder, the amount can be double to the proposed amount. And it has to be dealt with the murder case.

4.11 Basis of Different Amounts of Compensation

One may say that the differences of amount of compensation can cause injustice in the face of equality. Of course, it is. Nevertheless, this is the method of judgment based on the term, 'similar and dissimilar actions', which is one of the characteristics of justice of compensation.[179] On this basis, it is opined that equality can be brought about according to the economic background of the rapists. Otherwise, it may become too burdensome for weaker sections of people by pursuing equality which may wipe out the injunction of justice. On the other hand, this is the adjustable method of judgment under Christian love.

4.12 Triumph of Justice of Compensation and Neighborly Love over the Rape Case

The success of justice of compensation and neighborly love starts from individual level. With reference to rape case, both rape victims

---

much they can afford. This is the panorama expected to portray justice in a flexible or adjustable manner with the condition of the people.

[177] Those who have huge amount deserve to pay more according to the principle of equality based on economic condition. For instance, leader like, BSP MLA of Utter Pradesh by name Purushottam Naresh Dwivedi who is reported to have raped a minor (Vide: 'FIR BSP MLA' for raping minor', in *The Times of India*, Bangalore, 13 January 2011, 9).

[178] If a stray lunatic rapes a girl, state government should be responsible rewarding the mentioned amount of compensation to the victim. However, if the lunatic is still with his family, the family should be responsible. However, the amount of the compensation should be conditional as it is.

[179] The characteristics of justice of compensation are described in the first chapter of this book.

and rapists become neighbors who are expected to help one another in time of hurt. This way, the responsibility of both forgiveness and compensation becomes a kind of help to one another simultaneously. Under this circumstance, there is no disappointment between them but compromise for the speedy recovery of relationship. In this way, there can be an immediate and lasting solution without much effort even though rape is a serious crime.

4.13 Conclusion

The nature of rape is normally wide ranging. It depends on culture, place and time. As a result, the legal definition of rape differs from state to state though the understanding mostly refers to penis-penetration. As per the understanding in India, IPC clearly notes it as 'without her consent'. This term is also clear enough because rape is an action against one individual and even against the state. Such act affects people starting from kid to aged. By the incident of rape, numbers of female were murdered brutally and many were injured physically, psychologically, spiritually and socially. In relation to this, though insufficiency hanged on many accused were fined and arrested to prison as punishment. In this manner, the number of rape case is increasing year by year instead of decreasing. Exclusively no one deserves to be blamed for this development except the structure and management of law and order in one way or the other. At this moment, I see that the structure of the law for any crime reflects punishment and the decision-making of criminal case based on justice alone, which is never separable with love. Therefore, I am inclined to apply the principles of justice of compensation and neighborly love from Christian perspective having the conviction to overcome those discrepancies in the decision-making. Under these principles, I propose five kinds of compensation to represent justice that there will be a speedy recovery between rape victim and rapist. At the same time, it is argued that such principles will also help both rape victim and rapist to experience true love through such painful situation.

Conclusion

The thrust of this book is to draw a relationship between retributive justice and ethics of love with reference to rape victim. The relations are drawn by positing with the hypothesis that there is no true love without retributive justice between rape victim and rapist. This hypothesis tries to establish the inextricable linkages between justice and love in crime. Here, using the method of 'Christian love' the principles of justice of compensation and neighborly love are applied from the Christian perspective on decision-making of any crime, particularly rape case. Here, it is also argued that the dimensions of justice and love are necessary in decision-making of crime.

From the points of justice, nowadays the structure of law and order especially for crime hardly draws attention on justice. For it is learnt that most of its structure is based on the law of retribution. As far as retributive justice is concerned, punishment is necessary for the evil act and for the sake of justice. Therefore, the nature of decision-making based on such theory expresses punishment as the consequence of evil deed. Solution is also based on the equality through the characteristic of retaliation that wipes out the picture of justice and love consecutively. From the points of love, it seems that such structure based on retributive justice values only justice as matter in the decision-making. It wipes away the image of love in the decision-making due punishment as the consequence of committed action. Overturning such nature of structure, love is accepted as the only way to decide everything in Christian approach especially the so-called 'evangelical approach', rooted in the theology, 'from above', which is opposite to the theology, 'from below'. By the law of love, forgiveness replaces the expression of punishment in any crime. Like this, many of the criminal laws hardly draw the relationship between justice and love nowadays. This is the very ground that I am confronted to inquire a way as a new approach that relates justice and love in the situation of crime. For which I apply the principles of justice of compensation and neighborly love under the method of 'Christian love'. Theoretically, their relationships focus on mutual and complimentary characteristics. Mutual characteristic deals with the conditions of 'damage' under justice of compensation and 'need' under neighborly love, and complimentary deals with the balance between spiritual and physical aspects that depend on each other. Practically, the relationships focus on the mid-point that determines the safety of victim and offender through help being neighbor to each other.

Such principles are very much needed nowadays, especially for the rape case in India. Rape is chosen because the decision-making in the law and order seems so fragmentary while it is continuously occurring in such a brutal way. Rape is not against an individual alone but against the state according to IPC. In such circumstance, the approach of decision-making for the case of rape is ambiguous. For instance, there is no sufficient rape compensation from government and other NGOs. Besides, there is no fix rate of compensation to be carried out by the rapist alone. Moreover, there are always negligence of security and manipulation of rape cases in the court. Of course, some forms of punishment like imprisonment, monetary compensation from government, NGOs, and even from rapist are being worked out to resolve the case. However, they are not based on justice but punishment for the evil act. As a result, people keep on grumbling that justice is denied to rape victim. Even if there is a kind of solution, it emphasizes on beyond rather than on the satisfaction of rape victim and rapist.

Therefore, it is necessary to apply the above principles in the case of rape to overthrow the characteristics of retributive justice, to elevate a norm for compensation by rapist and to decide the case at individual levels. In relation to this, five kinds of compensation are underlined to confront rape crime considered as benevolent services. Such is the standard expressed to decide the rape case set at the most possible and adjustable way. As law is made for the lawless and disobedient and not for the innocent per se, this standard would do well to deal with rapist. As long as crime remains, so will the relevance of this approach be.

Bibliography

Anderson, J. Kerby. *Moral Dilemmas: Biblical Perspectives on Contemporary Ethical Issues*. Nashville: Word Publishing. 1998.

Barth, Karl. *The Epistle to the Romans,* sixth ed., translated by Edwyn C. Hoskyns. London: Oxford University Press. 1933.

Bauckham, Richard and Benjamin Drewery. Eds. *Scripture, Tradition and Reason: A Study in the Criteria of Christian Doctrine.* Edinburgh: T & T Clark. 1988.

Brady, Bernerd V. *The Moral of Bond Community: Justice and Discourse in Christian Morality*. Washington D.C.: George Town University Press. 1998.

Carson, D.A. *Showing the Spirit: A Theological Exposition of I Corinthians 12-14*. Michigan: Baker Books. 1987.

Demant, V.A. *Christian Sex Ethics: An Introduction*. Evanston: Harper and Row Publishers. 1963.

Dietrich, Gabriele and Bas Wielenga. *Toward Understanding Indian Society*. Kottayam: Wigi Printers. 2003.

Flavia. Ed. *Journey to Justice: Procedures to be Followed in a Rape Case.* Mumbai: N.P. 1990.

Fortune, Marie M. *Sexual Violence: The Unmentionable Sin*. Ohio: The Pilgrim Press. 1983.

Furnish, Victor Paul. *The Love Command in the New Testament.* London: SCM Press Ltd. 1973.

Geetha, V. *Patriarchy: Theorizing Feminism.* Calcutta: Bhatkal and Sen. 2007.

Granberg-Michaelson, Karin. *Healing Community*. Geneva: WCC Publications. 1991.

Grenz, Stanley J. and Roger E. Olson. Eds. *20th Century Theology: God and the World in a Transitional Age*. Secunderabad: OM Books. 2004.

Gustafson, James Walter with Joseph B. Onyango-Okello. *The Quest for Truth: An Introduction to Philosophy.* Massachusetts: Proclaim Publication. 2007.

Harland, Gordon. Ed. *The Thought of Reinhold Niebuhr*. New York: Oxford University Press. 1960.

Hefner, Philip. *Three Essays.* Philadelphia: Fortress Press. 1972.

Hoskyns, Edwyn C. *The Epistle to the Romans.* Sixth ed. London: Oxford University Press. 1933.

Jackson, P. Timothy. *The Priority of Love: Christian Charity and Social Justice*. New Jersey: Princeton University Press. 2003.

Kant, Immanuel. *Religion within the Limits of Reason Alone.* New York: Harper and Row. 1960.

Kim, Wook Yong. Ed. *The Secrets of Forgiveness and Being Born Again 1.* Seoul: Good News Publishing House. 1997.

Kuttianimattathil, SDB, Jose. *Theological Anthropology: A Christian Vision of Human Beings.* New Delhi: Rekha Printers Pvt. Ltd. 2009.

LaVerdiere, S.S.S. Eugene *Luke: New Testament Message, Volume 5.* Minnesota: The Liturgical Press, 1990.

Mabry, Hunter. Ed. *Christian Ethics: An Introductory Reader.* Delhi: ISPCK. 2002.

Manson, T.W. *Ethics and the Gospel.* New York: SCM Press Ltd. 1960.

Marshall, Christopher D. *Beyond Retribution: A New Testament Vision for Justice, Crime and Punishment.* Sydney: Lime Grove House Publishing. 2001.

Marx, Karl. *Wages, Price and Profit: Workers of all Countries, Unite.* Peking: Foreign Languages Press. 1970.

McCabe, Herbert. *What is Ethics all About?* Washington: Corpus Publication, 1969.

McLaren, Robert Bruch. *Christian Ethics: Foundations and Practice.* New Jersey: Prentice Hall. 1994.

McQuilkin, Robertson. *An Introduction to Biblical Ethics.* Secunderabad: OM Books. 2002.

Moberly, Elizabeth. *Suffering Innocent and Guilty.* London: SPCK. 1978.

Moo, Douglas J. *The Letter of James.* Leicester: Apollos. 2000.

Muelder, Walter, G. *Moral Law in Christian Social Ethics.* Virginia: John Knox Press. 1966.

Outka, Gene H. and Paul Ramsey. Eds. *Norm and Context in Christian Ethics.* London: SCM Press Ltd. 1969.

Outka, Gene. *Agape: An Ethical Analysis.* Massachusetts: Alpine Press. 1972.

Pathil, Kuncheria and Dominic Veliath, *An Introduction to Theology: Indian Theological Series.* New Delhi: Rekha Printers Pvt. Ltd. 2003.

Patterson, Bob E. *Friedrich Schleiermacher.* Texas: Word Books Publisher. 1979.

Perlewitz, M.M., Miriam. *The Gospel of Matthew.* Wilmington: Michael Glazier Inc. 1988.

Pixley, George V. *On Exodus: A Liberation Perspective.* New York: Orbis Books. 1987.

Pritchard, James B. *An Ancient Near East Texts Relating to the Old Testament.* New Jersey: Princeton University Press. 1955.

Quinney, Richard. *Class, State and Crime.* Second edition. London: Longman Inc. 1980.

Qureshi, M.U. *Women and Crime.* New Delhi: Chaman Enterprises. 2006.

Ramsey, Paul. *Basic Christian Ethics.* London: SCM Press Ltd. 1950.

Ramsey, Paul. *Deeds and Rules in Christian Ethics:* Scottish Journal of Theology Occasional Paper No.11. London: Oliver and Boyd. 1967.

Reiman, Jeffrey. *Justice and Modern Moral Philosophy.* London: Yale University Press. 1990.

Rowland, Jr, Stanley J. *Ethics, Crime and Redemption: Christian Perspectives on Social Problems.* Philadelphia: The Westminster Press. N.D.

Schleiermacher, Friedrich. *The Christian Faith.* Second ed. Edinburgh: T & T Clark. 1948.

Schwartz, Pepper and Virginia Rutter. *The Gender of Sexuality.* New Delhi: Pine Forge Press. 1998.

Sharma, K.L. *Social Stratification in India.* New Delhi: Sage Publications. 1997.

Sharma, Manish. Ed. *When the Fathers Rape: A Socio-psycho-legal-global Study.* New Delhi: A.P.H. Publishing Corporation. 1996.

Solomon, Robert C. and Mark C. Murphy. Eds. *What is Justice: Classic and Contemporary Readings.* New York: Oxford University Press. 1990.

Storrar, William F. and Andrew R. Morton. Eds. *Public Theology for the 21st Century.* New York: T & T Clark. 2004.

Sutherland, Edwin H. and Donald R. Cressey. Eds. *Principles of Criminology.* Sixth edition. New York: J.B. Lippincott Company. 1960.

Tate, W. Randolph. *Interpreting the Bible: A Handbook of Terms and Methods.* Massachusetts: Hendrickson Publishers, Inc. 2006.

Thekkinedath, Joseph. *Love of Neighbour in Mahatma Gandhi.* Bangalore: St. Paul Press Training School. 1973.

Tillich, Paul. *Love Power and Justice: Ontological Analysis and Ethical Application.* New York: Oxford University Press. 1954.

Townsend, Michael J. *The Epistle of James.* London: Epworth Press. 1989.

Turner, Philip. Ed. *Men and Women: Sexual Ethics in Turbulent Times.* Massachusetts: Cowley Publications. 1989.

Vanier, Jean. *Jesus, the Gift of Love.* New York: The Crossroad Publishing Company. 1994.

Webster, John. *Karl Barth.* London: Biddles Ltd. 2000.

Wood, Christ. *The End of Punishment: Christian Perspective on the Crisis in Criminal Justice.* Edinburgh: Saint Andrew Press. 1991.

Wright, Christopher J. H. *An Eye for an Eye: The Place of Old Testament Ethics Today.* Illinois: InterVarsity Press. 1983.

Wright, Tom. *Mark for Everyone.* London: Westminster John Knox Press. 2004.

Wyschogrod, Edith and Gerald P. McKenny. Eds. *The Ethical.* Berlin: Blackwell Publishing Ltd. 2003.

Dictionaries

Bowden, Alan Richardson John. Ed. *The Westminster Dictionary of Christian Theology.* Philadelphia: The Westminster Press. 1983.

Ferguson, Sinclair B. and David F. Wright. Eds. *New Dictionary of Theology.* Illinois: InterVarsity Press. 1998.

Hastings, James. Ed. *Dictionary of the Bible.* Sixth printing. New York: Hendrickson Publishers. Inc. 2005.

Commentaries

Anderson, J. Kerby. *Moral Dilemmas: Biblical Perspectives on Contemporary Ethical Issues.* Nashville: Word Publishing. 1998.

Cassuto, U. *A Commentary on the Book of Exodus.* Jerusalem: The Magnes Press. 1967.

Cole, R. Alan. Ed. *Exodus: An Introduction and Commentary.* London: InterVarsity Press. 1973.

Morris, Canon Leon. *Luke: An Introduction and Commentary.* Revised edition. Michigan: InterVarsity Press. 2000.

Wright, Christopher J.H. *Deuteronomy: New International Biblical Commentary*. Massachusetts: Hendrickson Publishers. Inc. 1996.

Encyclopedia

Brill, Eerdmans. Ed. *The Encyclopedia of Christianity,* vol. 5, (Si-Z). Boston: William B. Eerdmans Publishing Company. 2008.

Report

Human Rights Violations against Sexuality Minorities in India. *Fact-finding Report about Bangalore* (A PUCL-K). N.D.

Research

Multiple Action Research Group, *Rape Kidnapping and Abduction: Our Laws 9.* New Delhi: Print Art. 1992.

Unpublished Articles

A Lesser Child: Girl Child in India. Readings on Women Studies Series: 7. Bombay: Research Centre for Women's Studies at Shreemati Nathibai Damodar Thackersey Women's University. N.D.

Women and Rape. Pune: Streevani Documentation Centre – 1991 – 1993. 16.

Webliographies

http:cvaconline.org/resources/thefinalthesis.pdf. (17 December 2010).

http//desicritics.rog/2010/03/27/065314.php. (6 January 2011).

http://family.jrank.org/pages/1350/Rape-Causes-Rape.html (12 February 2011).

http://en.wikipedia.org/restorativejustice . (12 December 2010).

(http://news.ninemsn.com.au/national/1075801/taxpayers-pay-compensation-for-broke-rapist. (6 January 2011).

http://www.backlash.com/book/rape6.html (16 February 2011).

http://www.backlash.com/book/rape6.html (13 February 2011).

http://www.denverspiritualcommunity.org/Wisdom/Mastership5htm. (17 December 2010).

http://www.direct.gov.uk/enCrimeJusticeAndTheLaw/VictimsOf Crime/DG_177421. (17 December 2010).

http://www.johnhoward.ab.ca/pub/pdf/c27.pdf. (12 December 2010).

(http://www.punjabnewsline/com/content/punjab-pat-rs30000-conpensation-rape-victims/27467. (6 January 2011).

Newspapers

The Times of India (Bangalore), 25 November 2010.

The Times of India (Bangalore), 18 December 2010.

The Times of India (Bangalore), 21 December 2010.

The Times of India (Bangalore), 11 February 2011.

The Times of India (New Delhi), 2 February 2013.